A ~
Journey
into
Prayer

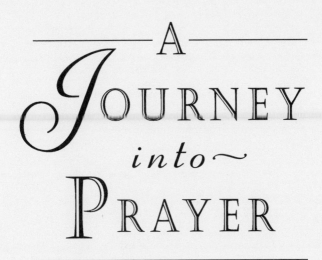

A Journey into~ Prayer

Evelyn Christenson

COMPILED BY SARAH M. PETERSON

Chariot VICTOR
PUBLISHING
A DIVISION OF COOK COMMUNICATIONS

All Scripture quotations, unless indicated, are taken from the *Holy Bible, New International Version®*. Copyright © 1973, 1978, 1984 by International Bible Society. Used by permission of Zondervan Publishing House. All rights reserved. Other quotations are taken from the *New American Standard Bible* (NASB), © the Lockman Foundation, 1960, 1962, 1963, 1968, 1971, 1972, 1973, 1975, 1977; the *King James Version* (KJV); and *The Living Bible* (TLB), © 1971, Tyndale House Publishers, Wheaton, IL 60189. Used by permission.

This book contains adaptations from the following books by Evelyn Christenson: *What Happens When Women Pray, Battling the Prince of Darkness,* and *What Happens When God Answers Prayer.*

Editor: Sarah M. Peterson
Designer: Andrea Boven
Cover Photo: Tony Stone Images

Victor Books is an imprint of ChariotVictor Publishing, a division of Cook Communications, Colorado Springs, Colorado 80918
Cook Communications, Paris, Ontario
Kingsway Communications, Eastbourne, England

Library of Congress Cataloging-in-Publication Data

Christenson, Evelyn.
    A journey into prayer / by Evelyn Christenson, with Sarah M. Peterson.
        p. cm.
    Includes index.
    ISBN 1-56476-501-6
    1. Prayer—Christianity.   I. Peterson, Sarah M.   II. Title.
BV210.2.C525   1995
248.3'2—dc20   95-18469
                                                            CIP

CONTENTS

Dedicated to the dear, precious women
of my United Prayer Ministry Board
who have prayed for me faithfully
every day since 1973.

God has used their prayers to produce
my books for this devotional.

Introduction

Sarah Peterson has carefully and lovingly gleaned snapshots of my writings for this book. This collection of short word pictures on a myriad of subjects is intended to take you on a journey of prayer with me. Some are from days past, and some from just yesterday. But all are as fresh as prayer—which is new every morning.

Sarah's desire, and mine also, is that you will walk thoughtfully through some of them, skip for joy at others, and sometimes pause to reflect on what God is saying to you too. But we trust that always, as God speaks to your heart as He has to mine through His Word, you will hide the truths deep in your heart. And then you will find the victory of obeying, and the thrill of walking hand in hand with God—listening and talking to Him, your friend—and mine.

Thanks, Sarah!

Evelyn

When We Pray

Pray without ceasing.
1 Thessalonians 5:17, NASB

D id you ever sit in a room before a glowing fire with someone you love? Did you talk every minute? Or did you feel compelled every now and then to clear your throat and say, "Now, dear, I think I'll say something to you." Then with a bright introduction, did you proceed with a formal speech? Of course not. When you're with a person you love, there need not be a bit of conversation in order for you to experience real communication. If you feel like saying something, you do; if not, you don't; but the line of communication is always open.

Praying without ceasing is like that. How? It's simply turning the dial of our communication system with God to *On,* making possible a two-way conversation with Him at any time. When that communication line is open, we can say whatever we want to Him, and He in turn can say anything He wishes to us. Yes, it's possible to "pray without ceasing" twenty-four hours a day.

When we leave our daily closet praying, do we walk out and slam the door, saying, "That's it for today. Same time tomorrow, Lord, same station"? That isn't what the Holy Spirit meant when He inspired Paul to write, "Pray without ceasing" (1 Thessalonians 5:17, NASB). Nor is it what Christ meant when He taught His disciples, "Men ought always to pray, and not to faint" (Luke 18:1, NASB).

After Paul lists the armor with which we are to resist Satan, he goes on to say, "Pray in the Spirit on all occasions" (Ephesians 6:18). The source of strength in our battle with the enemy is "praying always." But when the line of communication with God closes, wham—the fiery darts of Satan strike! But that need not be the case. The communication system between God and us can be open all twenty-four hours.

> *Dear Lord, Thank You that You want us to be open to each other always. Help me to take advantage of this precious privilege and to keep my line of communication open to You at all times.*

First Priority: Prayer

Pray in the Spirit on all occasions
with all kinds of prayers and requests.
Ephesians 6:18

T hings can happen when we don't plan and just pray.

A long distance call came to our church one Sunday morning. It was an evangelist calling from California. "May I use your church building for a meeting on Tuesday night?" he asked. "You won't have to do a thing. I just want to reach some hippies for Christ."

My husband said, "Fine, you may use our church."

The evangelist arrived on Tuesday morning. There had been no time to advertise the meeting in local newspapers or in other churches. The only means of communication had been the hippie "underground" method. But Tuesday morning was our women's prayer meeting, and we had only one prayer — that somehow the hippies of the area would hear there was to be a meeting for them in our church that night.

As we were praying, our church secretary came flying downstairs and interrupted our prayer with, "The religion editor of our city's newspaper came to interview our speaker; now they're both on their knees praying!" The religion editor received Christ. The meeting had front-page coverage that evening. How else would you get such great newspaper advertising in a short time?

We had 1,100 hippies in our church that night. These characters, and I mean characters, came en masse to the service. When the invitation was given that night over 100 of them accepted Christ. As the Christians came forward to find a place to pray with these young people, there wasn't a closet, or a hallway, or a side room anywhere in the church where people weren't already praying!

On Sunday, my husband laid aside his prepared sermon and announced, "I can speak on only one subject this morning: 'What Happens When You Don't Plan, You Just Pray!' "

> *Lord, Help me to realize that prayer—
not plans and programs—is my most powerful tool.*

LORD, TEACH US TO PRAY

Lord, teach us to pray.
Luke 11:1

W e can learn from the Upper Room pray-ers in Acts 1. They were putting into practice what Jesus had taught them about prayer when He was on earth. His disciples must have felt a tremendous lack in their own lives as they saw the beautiful example of the prayer life of their Lord. In their need they cried, "Lord, teach us to pray" (Luke 11:1).

Today, earnest followers of the Lord sense their need just as the disciples did after Jesus ascended. It's amazing that we can knock on doors, get on the telephone, invite people to our prayer groups, only to find that when we meet together we do not know how to pray. I was one of eleven people who formed 5,000 prayer groups for a Billy Graham Crusade held in our area. Afterward we heard that fantastic things had happened in some of those prayer groups where women had prayed for five consecutive weeks before and during the crusade. But hundreds of women said to me, "We did everything you told us to do. We knocked on doors, we called our neighbors, We did all these things, but we didn't know what to do when we got together. We didn't know how to pray."

Jesus' response to His disciples and to us is simple, yet so beautiful: "When you pray, say, 'Our Father who art in heaven. . . .' " You recognize that, don't you? It's the beginning of what we sometimes call "The Lord's Prayer." What is prayer? *Real prayer is simply conversation with God our Father.* Jesus didn't say, "Now, when you pray, say, '*My* Father.' " No, He used the plural, "*Our* Father." He is your Father, my Father, Jesus' Father — "Our Father who art in heaven." It's so simple. Just conversation with God.

> ➤ *Dear Father, Teach me to pray*
> *simply by talking to You.*

BEFORE YOU PRAY FOR OTHERS...

Search me, O God, and know my heart. . . .
See if there is any offensive way in me.
Psalm 139:23-24

Everything seemed to be going great in our church. In four years our membership had almost doubled, a building program was in progress, and we had a full schedule of activities to meet the needs of our congregation. Yet, three of us sensed from God that there was a missing dimension. We decided to meet once a week to pray for our church—a very noble idea, we thought.

We agreed at the start to base our praying on a verse of Scripture—a good rule to follow—and right away God gave us Psalm 66:18: "If *I* regard iniquity in my heart, the Lord will not hear *me*" (NASB).

"Lord, what do You mean?" we asked. "We're going to pray for our church." But He continued to apply the pressure gently: "If I regard iniquity in my heart, the Lord will not hear me." Wow! I, the wife of a senior pastor? Uh huh.

God didn't release us to pray for other needs until we had cleaned up our own lives by confessing our sins. We prayed and prayed, and God kept bringing sins and sins to our minds. As our first prayer meeting came to a close, we thought, *Phew! We got that one over with; next week we can start praying for the needs of the church.* But when we met the following week, we still couldn't get beyond Psalms 66:18! God kept bringing our wrong priorities, thoughts, reactions, and attitudes to our minds. It took us weeks—six whole weeks—to get out of Psalm 66:18 and into effectual fervent praying for the church.

> ➤ *Dear Father, Help me to recognize*
> *what You call sin in my life,*
> *so that I may confess it to You.*

Pray First, Plan Later

The prayer of a righteous man
is powerful and effective.
James 5:16

G od expects us to be orderly. He expects us to manage our time, to discipline ourselves, to prepare well-planned programs. But if we could learn to pray first and plan afterward, how different would be our homes, our churches, our Christian clubs, our Bible studies, whatever we are doing for Christ. Maybe, just maybe, we are planning in one direction and God's will is in another direction. God might say, "Hold everything! Turn around and go this way. This is My will for you, not that way."

Even if we are plugged into God's will and know we're going in the right direction, we may be going at a snail's pace. God says, "Look, you see only a tenth of what I have for you. There are nine-tenths that you're not seeing, that you don't know anything about."

God wants us to make ourselves available to Him, and to say before we start to plan, "Lord, tell me what You want me to do, where You want me to go, how You want me to do it." Then our omnipotent God, with all the abundance of heaven at His disposal, will pour out His power upon us. Instead of following our tiny, tiny plans, God wants to open heaven and flood us. It's exciting.

We work, we pull, we struggle, and we plan until we're utterly exhausted, but we have forgotten to plug into the source of power. And that source of power is prayer—the fervent prayer of a righteous person that is powerful and effective.

> *Dear God, Teach me to plug into Your power instead of just my limited human resources. Amen.*

Thanking God in All Things

Praise the Lord, O my soul, and forget not all His benefits.
He forgives all my sins and heals all my disease;
He redeems my life from the pit
and crowns me with love and compassion.
He satisfies my desires with good things so that my youth
is renewed like the eagle's.

Psalm 103:2-5

Ephesians 5:20 says that God expects us to be thankful for His answer, no matter how He answers our prayer—even when it is not what we wanted. "Always giving thanks *for* all things in the name of our Lord Jesus Christ to God, even the Father" (NASB). Then *always* giving thanks every time—even when we had asked for something different. His answers are the source of our praise and thanks, no matter how our opinions differ from God's.

A friend wrote me a note several years ago in which she expressed her thanks to the Lord for a pair of crutches! She had just completed thirty years with the Back to the Bible broadcasts when she wrote, "I fell, broke my ankle in three places, and dislocated the bone. Surgery was necessary

... but I even find myself thanking the Lord for crutches!"

I'm sure that another reason why we don't thank God *for* His answer is that frequently we don't recognize events and gifts as answers to our prayers. We just take His bountiful supply or dramatic action for granted when it comes. This is why I teach my prayer seminar participants to jot down their prayer request and then what happened so they can put the two together. Often I hear their surprised, "Oh, that *was* God's answer!"

Even worse, of course, is when God answers and we have forgotten that we even prayed. Keeping a list of our requests helps tremendously here, also. Then a periodic reading through the list of requests can be quite revealing: "Oh, yes, that provision, healing, or circumstance really *was* an answer to one of my prayers!" Then the thankfulness for it comes.

There are also those times when I believe God deliberately waits long enough to answer so that there will be no doubt who gets the credit for what happens. It is only when I have exhausted all human resources that He finally answers—so that I will recognize the answer as coming from Him. And thank Him for it. And give Him all the glory.

➤ *Lord, Thank You for Your answers that I recognized; but most of all, thanks for the things I never realized came from You!*

Private Prayer–
Public Praying

When you pray, go into your room, close the door and
pray to Your Father, who is unseen. Then Your Father,
who sees what is done in secret, will reward you.
Matthew 6:6

D o you have a secret place for private prayer, a certain corner, a particular chair, or a room set apart where you can spend time alone with God? A "closet" where you daily *shut the door* to pray to your Father in secret? The group concept of prayer is important, and we do need to pray with one another, "not giving up meeting together" (see Hebrews 10:25). But the drawing apart to pray in secret is perhaps the most vital type of prayer in which we engage. It is also an indicator of the kind of prayer group participant we really are, for it is our private praying that determines the quality and validity of our public praying.

Though we are never to be critical of the prayers of others, it is easy to recognize in our prayer groups those who have spent time in private closet prayer and the others who have come perhaps to do the only praying that they have done all week. Some struggle and strain to sound pious, but it's obvious that they haven't experienced the deeper dimension of closet prayer.

Have you ever seen a bright blue iceberg? In Alaska I stared in awe at a mountain lake filled with beautiful blue icebergs that had broken off Portage Glacier. Immediately my mind went back to an article in a *Family Tie* magazine that compared our secret praying to an iceberg. The "Absolutely No Boating" sign on the edge of the lake reminded me that eight-ninths of the bulk of an iceberg is below the waterline—out of sight. Only one-ninth is visible above the surface. The next day at our prayer seminar in Anchorage I explained how prayer should be like those icebergs, with about one-ninth showing in our public group praying and eight-ninths out of sight in our secret closets.

> *Dear Father, I want to be close to You.*
Help me to maintain discipline in my private prayer
life so that I will mature and grow nearer to You daily.

Me? . . . Sin?

*If we claim to be without sin, we deceive ourselves
and the truth is not in us.*
1 John 1:8

S omeone once asked me, "What kinds of sins
does someone like you commit, or is that too
personal?"

Not knowing how to answer her offhand, I decided to compile a list of the many sins I had confessed with the help of a former prayer partner.
Together, we remembered the sins we struggled
with.

"The main one I remember," she said, "was our
superior attitude concerning our spiritual status
compared to others, and the idea that we should
pray *for* them. God showed us that attitude was
sin." (I added that one to the two-page list I had
jotted down in answer to the question!) What other
sins did we have to confess?

• Divided motives. We were very involved in
serving Christ, thinking our reasons were all for His
glory. But God showed us how much there was of
ego, self-fulfillment, self-satisfaction, and desire to
build up our own worth in the eyes of our fellow
church members.

• **Pretense.** My prayer partner had confessed that she wasn't the mature, godly woman everyone thought she was. People had her on a pedestal; and she didn't dare admit, even to her family, that she wasn't as spiritual as everybody told her she was.

• **Pride.** How surprised I was when God exposed as sin the slight feeling of "Look what I've done" that would come over me as I passed the copies of my original lesson outline to the members of my adult Sunday School class.

Neither of us had been practicing the "dirty dozen" sins, but God exposed one by one the "little Christian sins" that Peter could have been referring to when he wrote "For the eyes of the Lord are on the righteous, and His ears are open to their prayers, but the face of the Lord is against those who do evil" (1 Peter 3:12).

> ➤ *Dear Father, I confess as sin whatever*
> *You bring to my mind.*

WHEN GOD ANSWERS

. . . set your hearts on things above,
where Christ is seated at the right hand of God.
Set your minds on things above, not on earthly things.
Colossians 3:1-2

When God answers a prayer, it is not the final closing curtain on an episode in our lives. Rather, it is the opening of the curtain to the next act. The most important part of prayer is what we do with God's answers and how His answers affect us.

God never intends that an answer to prayer be an end in itself. He expects much more than an emotional response — joy, disappointment, or anger — to His answer. He expects us to be prepared to act or to be acted upon by His answer to our prayers.

God's answer to a prayer is His means of accomplishing His will here on Earth. The way He answers reveals to us His sovereign will, His plan, His reasoning, and His perspective on the subject. We must ask, "What does God expect to accomplish *with* this answer?"

We seem to place so much emphasis on our prayer requests, and then on God's answers, that we forget what He intends us to do *with* His answers. Most of us pray a specific prayer, receive an answer—whether or not it is to our liking—and consider the case closed. In our prayer notebooks, we write down the request, and then opposite it—with joyous or resigned finality—record the answer when it comes. But God does not consider the case closed. He opens a whole new area of action by the answer He gives. Our response to His answer should be, "What next, Lord?"

According to Jeremiah 33:3, there is another step, something *after* the prayer and *after* the answer:

Call unto Me, *and* I will answer thee, *and* show thee great and mighty things, which thou knowest not (KJV, emphasis added).

God's time-tested promise to Jeremiah is in three parts, not our usual two-part approach of "our calling" and "His answering."

Rarely does God stamp "case closed" when He answers one of our prayers. Rather, it is often what happens *after* God answers that is life-changing.

➤ *Dear Father, Help me to be wise*
with the way I handle Your answers to my prayers.
I want to set my mind and heart on things above.

THE PLACE OF PRAISE

. . . always giving thanks to God the Father
for everything, in the name of our Lord Jesus Christ.
Ephesians 5:20

W e may reach the place suddenly, or it may take us years to realize that God isn't making a mistake in our lives. But then we are at the point where we can praise Him. A new Christian in my Bible study called me one day and said, "Mrs. Chris, I think I found a wrong translation in the Bible. It's there in the first chapter of James, verse 2. Isn't it wrong when it says, 'Consider it pure joy, my brothers, whenever you face trials of many kinds'?"

I smiled over the phone and said, "No, Honey, it's not wrong. This is the place you reach when after years and years of trials and difficulties, you see that all has been working out for your good, and that God's will is perfect. You see that He has made no mistakes. He knew all of the 'what ifs' in your life. When you finally recognize this, even during the trials, it's possible to have joy, deep down joy."

Philippians 4:6 comes into focus at this point: "Do not be anxious about anything, but by prayer and petition, with thanksgiving, present your requests to God." It is a privilege to see God being glorified in our lives. We are to give thanks always, knowing that we have a God who never makes a mistake. And if we are going to be effectual intercessory pray-ers, praying in the will of God, it's not something we tack on to the end of our prayers. It's a commitment to God's will, a way of life. It's being willing for His will in the things for which we are praying and in our personal lives. And it's "always giving thanks to God the Father for everything, in the name of our Lord Jesus Christ" (Ephesians 5:20). This is easier said than done—but the rewards are fantastic!

> *Lord, I know that my attitude isn't as thankful as it should be. Please give me that spirit which rejoices in all things.*

SIN AND THE CHRISTIAN

If we confess our sins, He is faithful and
just and will forgive us our sins
and purify us from all unrighteousness.
1 John 1:9

After we become Christians we commit sins. What do we do with them? Do we live with them? The answer is that we get rid of them. God gives Christians the formula: "If *we* confess *our* sins, He is faithful and just to forgive us *our sins,* and to cleanse us from all unrighteousness" (1 John 1:9, emphasis added). This Scripture is written only to Christians to tell us how we may be cleansed and ready for an effectual intercessory prayer life.

Even little sins can muddy up our communication system. We try to get through to God and there's something in the way. It may be an attitude, a spoken word. God wants these things cleared up. He doesn't want anything between Him and us. If there is, it's our fault, not His, when His ears are closed to our prayers.

One dear woman objected to this. She said, "I don't like this one bit, this cleaning up of my life before I can be a good, strong, powerful intercessory pray-er."

Another countered, "Not me. I have preschool twin boys, and no matter how much I clean up my life before I start for this prayer meeting, by the time I reach here with them in the car, there's some attitude I have to get cleaned up before I can pray for others."

I found out later that the one who objected so strenuously was harboring a grave sin in her life. She didn't like this process, but it's very definite in God's Word. This, then, is the first prerequisite — nothing between God and ourselves when we approach intercessory prayer.

> ➤ *Thank You, Lord, for cleansing me from the sins I just confessed as You promised in 1 John 1:9 and qualifying me for effectual, intercessory prayer.*

FORGIVEN AS WE FORGIVE

*And forgive us our sins, just as we have forgiven
those who have sinned against us.*
Matthew 6:12, TLB

A dimension of prayer that Christ taught which is frequently overlooked by those seeking a deeper prayer life relates to the thing that is *most apt to break up your prayer group* — your relationship with other people who are in that group!

In the Lord's Prayer we read, "And forgive us our sins just *as* we have forgiven those who have sinned against us" (Matthew 6:12, TLB). Your Bible translation may say debts or trespasses; both have the same literal meaning: sins. If you want to keep your prayer group and other relationships intact, practice this principle.

That word *as* is a conditional word meaning "to the extent that" — to the extent that I forgive others, I'm asking God to forgive me.

Christ explained it like this: "For if you forgive men when they sin against you, your Heavenly Father will also forgive you. But if you do not forgive men their sins, your Father will not forgive your sins" (Matthew 6:14-15).

Christ says that if we don't forgive others, our

Heavenly Father will not forgive us. If He does not, then our unforgiven sins will keep Him from hearing our intercessory prayers. They will be of no avail.

So, unless we keep our relationships with other people clear, we cannot be effective intercessory pray-ers. God hears our plea for forgiveness of sins, but for us to refuse to forgive others is a sin. We can't be right with God and effective intercessors if we harbor the sin of an unforgiving spirit.

Jesus also admonished His disciples, in rather strong words, "Therefore I tell you, whatever you ask for in prayer, believe that you have received it, and it will be yours. And when you stand praying, if you hold anything against anyone, forgive him, so that your Father in heaven may forgive you your sins" (Mark 11:24-25).

➤ *Dear Father, Help me to forgive all who have sinned against me, so that You will forgive my sins—making me eligible for a right relationship with You.*

Righteous before the Lord

The prayer of a righteous man is powerful and effective.

James 5:16

T he prayer of a righteous man is powerful and effective." (James 5:16) A righteous person. It is his prayer, and only his, that is powerful and effective. If we are living in sin and liking it, if we are keeping it there, finding that it feels kind of good, if we're regarding—nurturing, patting that little sin along—God does not hear us. The Prophet Isaiah gives a powerful description of someone in this plight:

> Listen now! The Lord isn't too weak to save you. And He isn't getting deaf! He can hear you when you call! But the trouble is that your sins have cut you off from God. Because of sin He has turned His face away from you and will not listen anymore (Isaiah 59:1-2, TLB).

Do you wonder why your prayers aren't answered? Here is a possible reason: sin (or sins) in your life. It is "the prayer of a righteous [person that] is powerful and effective." If your prayers aren't bringing in results, this may be the reason.

Your problem may not be sins, but sin. And this is a very important point. When our Lord was talking to His disciples just before His crucifixion, He told them that He was going to send the Comforter, the Holy Spirit, who would convict the world—those who were not Christ's followers—of "sin, because men do not believe in Me" (John 16:9). *This is the sin that will keep God from hearing intercessory prayer—the sin of not believing in Christ as your personal Savior.* If this is your sin, the only prayer from you that God promises to hear is one of seeking Him and then repentance and faith as you invite Christ into your life.

➢ *Dear Father, I'm not sure my sin of not having accepted Jesus has ever been forgiven. Please forgive me and, Jesus, come into my life as my Savior—and my Lord.*

Finding Your
Prayer Closet

. . . Jesus often withdrew to lonely places and prayed.
Luke 5:16

I can almost hear you saying, "I can't spend great periods of my time in a closet." No, neither can I sometimes, but I have found another kind of closet praying. It's just drawing apart to God wherever I am—at the kitchen sink, at a desk, or even in a room filled with people.

"You must have tremendous power of concentration," someone said.

No, I've just learned to draw apart from people to God. Practicing this at a California retreat with 525 people packed in a room that barely held 500, we found, though touching elbows physically, that we could each draw apart mentally to God. This too is closet praying, though it is no substitute for drawing apart to that one spot, at that one time of the day, when we really spend time with God and His Word.

One of my very favorite "closets" is my car. As I draw apart, you may be sure I don't take my hands off the wheel, fold them, and kneel. To shut my eyes would be even worse!

Even a plane seat can be a prayer closet. For two years I had been praying with a friend about her sister who did not know Christ. Every time my friend wrote to her sister, she'd call asking me to pray for God to work in her heart as she received the letter. One day my plane had a ten-minute layover in a Midwestern city with no time to disembark. I looked out over that city and thought, "That's where my friend's sister lives!" Suddenly there descended from God a heavy, overwhelming burden to pray for her. I sat in that plane in the very depths of intercessory prayer. Two days later my elated friend called to say, "I just received a letter from my sister, and she accepted Christ!" When? The exact day God had said in that plane, "Evelyn, pray."

➤ *Lord, Show me all the places You want me to draw apart mentally and pray.*

A Lark or an Owl?

They were also to stand every morning to thank
and praise the LORD. They were to do the same
in the evening. . . .
1 Chronicles 23:30

How do you start your day? Are you a lark or an owl? Larks twitter and sing in the morning, but by the end of the day they're not doing too well, they have slowed down considerably. Owls take a little longer to get going in the morning, but gain momentum as the night progresses.

We're divided at our house. I'm a lark and my husband is definitely an owl. When we pray together at night and Chris prays on and on, I sometimes have to say, "Hurry up, Chris; you're losing me." But in the morning it's a different story. Chris groans and often feels like, "Right now I don't love anybody, but when I start loving again, you'll be first on the list." He pulls the covers up tighter when I shake him to tell him some great gem that I've just gotten from the Lord.

Because our individual, built-in clocks function differently, I've learned that there are no spiritual brownie points for being a lark. Is it possible our Heavenly Father created some of us to be larks and some to be owls so He would have somebody on the alert all twenty-four hours of the day?

When I'm asked, "How do you get all those messages ready? How can you possibly write so many? I have to reply, "I don't write messages, but I keep a notebook on my bedstand at all times. Then lying there communing with my Heavenly Father early in the morning, I just jot down whatever He says to me."

When I awaken, I say, "Lord, here I am. What do You want to say to me?" I write down the thoughts He gives me and keep them in file folders. Then when I put those papers in outline form, it's astounding to learn that God has given me every single thought I'll ever need — in time!

It's a very exciting procedure to wait upon God early in the morning while my mind is fresh, before anyone else comes on the scene, or before the "tyranny of the urgent" rushes in. Have you learned to say in the morning, "Lord, here I am. You tell me what You want me to know today, what You want me to do"? Have you asked Him, "Is there someone You want me to call? What do You have in mind for me today?" You'll be amazed at His answers!

> Dear Father, Teach me to meet You first
in the morning, so my day will start —
and finish — with Your directing.

In One Accord

They all joined together constantly in prayer. . . .
Acts 1:14

I t would be good if we could learn the prayer method that God has given to us from the Bible, the method of praying in one accord in small groups. How is this achieved? Simply by praying about only one subject at a time with one person praying aloud while the others in the group are praying silently on the same subject. In this way everyone is praying together, in one accord, instead of planning their other prayers in advance.

Have you ever been in a group when someone is praying a long prayer? And have you found that you were not really praying along with that person? Instead, you were mulling over in your mind all the things you were going to pray about when your turn came? I have, and my thoughts have run like this, "Lord, now bring to my mind. . . . Oh, I don't want to forget that one. . . . Say, that's a good request. . . . Thank You, Lord, for reminding me of that one." Then I have gone back and reviewed the prayer subjects on my fingers. Next, I've wondered what my introductory statement should be, or how I should conclude my prayer. While someone else has been praying, I have been planning my own long prayer in advance, instead of praying silently on the same subject with the person who is praying audibly. That's not praying in one accord.

You see, if everyone in a group is praying in one accord with the person who is praying aloud, the total number of prayers ascending to heaven is multiplied by the number who are praying silently. How much more power there is in prayer when all the participants are praying in one accord!

> ➤ *Father, Teach me to pray in one accord*
> *with other people, while they are praying audibly,*
> *so that You will hear both their prayers and mine.*

GOD SPEAKS IN THE SILENCE

Be still, and know that I am God.
Psalm 46:10

Silent periods between prayers are a privilege and a blessing. Don't panic when there's a lull—just listen! Prayer is a two-way conversation with God.

Today silence is almost a lost art. After a few seconds pass without audible prayer, someone usually feels compelled to clear her throat, shuffle her feet, or nervously finger a songbook. Somehow we think we have to talk at God all of the time, but there are marvelous things God wants to say to us. He has answers to our questions, secrets He wants to share, and yet we bombard Him with our "much praying." We forget that God is on His throne in heaven just waiting to say something great to us, if we would only give Him a chance. How frustrated He must be (if God can become frustrated) when He has something so wonderful to tell you and me, and we aren't quiet long enough to listen to what He has to say.

One day when I asked my son about a girl who lives near us, he said, "Oh, I guess she's fine, Mom, if she'd ever keep still so we would find out."

"What do you mean?" I asked.

"Well, on the school bus that girl talks every single minute. She might be a real great girl, but she doesn't shut up long enough for us to find out."

Has God ever thought that about me? About you? Have we learned to keep still long enough for God to say something to us? It is in the *silence* that our communication becomes two-way.

> ➤ *Dear Father, Teach me to listen to*
> *Your voice in the silence.*

HOLY PLACES

The LORD is near to all who call on Him,
to all who call on Him in truth.
Psalm 145:18

God does not dwell in temples made with hands. Even so, some spots have been used as closets for prayer by so many that they seem to be holy places. Have you ever stepped into a room and felt God there? My husband and I were looking over the grounds at a Midwestern retreat center one fall. We stepped into an old chapel — and I felt God's presence immediately. "Hon, please go on without me for a few minutes," I said. I knelt at that altar — not talking or praying, but just *feeling* God so powerfully there.

Another time I arrived at Bethel Seminary in St. Paul to speak at a women's retreat just as the planning committee stepped out of the Eric Frykenberg Prayer Tower, where they had been praying. Their eyes were wide with wonder and amazement. "We felt Jesus in there!"

"Yes," I replied, "that is one of those places where I always feel a particular sense of the presence of Christ." That little circular room has no windows or furniture, but it is filled with the thousands of prayers uttered by students and faculty of that seminary—and Jesus' presence!

Christ recognized the need for spending time alone with God. What a tremendous example Christ's prayer life was to His followers and to us. Though the disciples were Jesus' very closest friends, He knew there were times He had to pray in secret to His Heavenly Father. Although Christ taught His disciples the concept of group prayer, He also knew the importance of this private closet praying. Even though He Himself was God incarnate, He thought it necessary to withdraw to a mountain to pray all night before the important task of choosing the twelve apostles. If He, why not us?

> *Lord, Keep me faithful to shut the door every day and spend time with You and Your Word in secret. Teach me to draw apart alone with You, no matter where I am or with whom.*

THINGS YOU
DO NOT KNOW

"Call to Me, and I will answer you,
and I will tell you great and mighty things,
which you do not know."
Jeremiah 33:3, NASB

H ave you ever wished that you could get a glimpse into God's mind? The God who ordained all the physical laws of space and time? The God who designed all the minute details of an incredibly complex universe? The God in whom all things consist and operate? There is a way. It is possible to perceive what is in the mind of the omniscient God of the universe. How? By examining His answers to your prayers!

In our prayer ministry, we have been continuously surprised at God's "things we did not know." As we have experimented for twenty-one years with ever-enlarging amounts and methods of prayer, God has surprised us with so much more than that for which we asked. I am constantly amazed that God does not limit answering our prayers because of our inability to ask.

The exciting thing is that the last phrase of Jeremiah 33:3 refers to things we know nothing about—

not ideas we dreamed up or plans we devised. As I look back over my life of prayer, this pattern becomes so obvious. I ask God for just one thing, and He keeps on answering long after I even recognize it as His response to my prayer.

Yes, each answer to prayer is God's opening of the door to what He intends to accomplish next in this world. With the answer to the initial prayer comes the continuation of God's involvement. But we may not recognize it as such; we may even forget that we prayed, or even worse, take for granted that what is happening is just the natural course of events. "Great and mighty things, which you do not know."

> ➤ *Lord, I want to recognize the way*
> *You answer my prayers. I don't want to take*
> *Your mysterious ways for granted.*

PRIORITIES

. . . as though God were making His appeal through us.
We implore you on Christ's behalf: Be reconciled to God.
2 Corinthians 5:20

On a blustery March morning during my devotions, I was "praying through" God's removing of all sin from me. Then, knowing He never leaves me as a fragile, empty shell from which He has removed these sins but that He then fills me, I started to tell Him all the things I knew I needed from Him. But suddenly, I changed my mind. "No, Lord, not what I think I need. This morning, would You please fill me with what's burdening You? Lord, what is Your number one priority for me today?" And immediately, before my mind's eye were two huge words, almost as if written in capital letters: WIN SOULS!

I often question why we spend so much time in our church prayer meetings praying for sick Christians who, if they die — and they will eventually — will go to be with Jesus, but we spend almost no time praying for the sinners who, when they die, will go to a Christless eternity.

Speaking at the Wednesday night prayer meeting in a famous church known for its deep spirituality, I mentioned in passing the appalling content of our church prayer lists. When the time came for group prayer, the interim pastor stood, holding a stack of church prayer sheets in his hands. Then, blushing, he stammered, "I'm ashamed to hand these out." And for good reason. All but one request was for sick people. Please don't stop praying for your sick members but *add* all those who are dying without Christ—lost—unreconciled to God.

God, in giving us the ministry of reconciliation, has made us ambassadors for Christ. It is "as though God were making His appeal *through* us. We implore you on Christ's behalf: Be reconciled to God" (2 Corinthians 5:20, emphasis mine).

> *Lord, I need to get back into focus.*
> *Help me to remember that winning souls*
> *for You is my top priority.*

GOD'S PERSPECTIVE OF ANSWERS TO PRAYER

*The God who made the world and everything in it
is the Lord of heaven and earth and does not live
in temples built by hands. And He is not served by
human hands, as if He needed anything, because He
Himself gives all men life and breath and everything else.*
Acts 17:24-25

There are surprises when God answers our prayers. I have discovered how "unhuman" God's ways of thinking really are. Things that seem so right, so good, so timely, so logical, so obvious to us frequently are refused, replaced, and even reversed by God as He—without ever making a mistake, missing the mark, being too early or too late—fields the answers out of His omniscient mind.

We need to see prayer from God's perspective. We should try to see the big picture of what God's overall plan might be and how each little and big request with His answer fits into His sovereign purpose. How often we question when God doesn't answer the way we wanted. How we grumble when we think He has not answered, when actually we have not recognized His answer. Or, when in rebellion, we decide that if this is how God is going to answer, we are never going to pray again.

But God has told us the "great and mighty things" He would do after His answers were "things we know not." God's omniscient thought process determines His answer to the prayers His earthly children pray, as well as all things those answers initiate.

Also, God's answer usually precipitates expanded and more fervent prayers from us. With His answer, we find ourselves on the next plateau from which we then launch our next endeavor through prayer.

How often we hear, "God always answers, but His answers are yes, no, or wait." In my own experience, I have not found God's answers to be that simplistic. His interaction with me in prayer is much more complete and far-reaching. His answer always includes, "Keep interacting with Me, My child. I have much I want to accomplish through your prayers."

➢ *Lord, Teach me to see things from Your perspective. I want to accomplish the plans You have prepared for me.*

Bear One
Another's Burdens

*Carry each other's burdens, and in this way
you will fulfill the law of Christ.*

Galatians 6:2

I s it as easy for your children to say, "Mom,
I'm having a math test at 10:30, please pray,"
as it is for them to ask you for $2.50 for lunch
money? Do your children know that your communication system with God is always open?

One morning while she was still in high school, one
of our daughters was so frightened about an upcom-
ing important interview that I found her sick to her
stomach in the bathroom. I helped her out the front
door and promised to pray. Soon the phone rang.
"Mother, it went great," she exclaimed, and then
softly, "I could *feel* you praying, Mom."

Our daughter Jan's father-in-law had just had
open-heart surgery. Suddenly the "Red Alert" was
flashed over the hospital intercom. Jan ran to a
phone, dialed our number and, with the sounds of
running hospital personnel in the background, said,
"Mother, Skip's dad's heart has stopped."

My heart stood still. I felt so helpless and so far
away. "What can I do?"

There was a long pause, and then she said, "Just pray, Mother, just pray," and hung up.

I did pray, and her father-in-law revived and God gave him four more years to live. But the point is that Jan knew she could depend on me to pray about her concerns, any time, any place.

This family prayer support works two ways. After finishing a retreat at Mt. Hermon, California, I phoned home long distance. My then ten-year-old son answered with, "How did it go, Mom?"

"Oh Kurt, it went just great."

"Well," he said with pride in his voice, "How could you miss with my whole pastor's class praying for you?"

Do you have someone who will pray for you and for whom you will pray? If you don't know where to start with all these prayer suggestions, find one person with whom you can share the secret problems and needs of your life. Someone who cares and who will never, never divulge your secrets. Then fulfill the law of Christ by "carry[ing] each other's burdens" (Galatians 6:2).

➤ *Lord, Give me a willing heart, so that I will always be available whenever someone needs me to pray. And I promise You I will pray.*

THE NIGHTWATCH

I thank God, whom I serve, as my forefathers did,
with a clear conscience, as night and day
I constantly remember you in my prayers.

2 Timothy 1:3

Are you one of these people whom God can awaken in the middle of the night to pray for one of His needs down here on Planet Earth? "But I need my sleep" you say. So did I, or at least I thought I did. For many years I was strictly hung up on sleeping pills—I thought I had to have eight solid hours of sleep or I'd never make it the next day. Then one summer day, I very undramatically tossed those pills into the toilet, flushed it, and said, "Lord, I'm not going to worry if I'm awake at night, because if You awaken me, there's a reason for it. I'll just ask You, 'For whom should I be praying?' "

God knows when I'm finished praying and ready to go back to sleep. And somehow there's no frustration and I never miss the sleep when God has needed me to pray. It's a very beautiful and exciting experience.

One night the Lord awoke me and said, "Pray for Jacque" (a long-time prayer partner). At that time she was in San Francisco, and I learned later that she was going through a very deep spiritual battle, seemingly surrounded by forces of Satan. A letter Jacque wrote to me the next morning confirmed the reason God had awakened me. As I prayed in St. Paul, great peace had flooded her in San Francisco. *If at night you can't sleep, don't count sheep — talk to the Shepherd!*

Is your communication system so open to God that you are available to pray any time of the day or night? When God sees a need down here on Planet Earth, can He say to you, "Wake up, wake up, I need you to pray for somebody"? Are you one of those with whom God can trust His burdens? Or are you like I was at one time, thinking you need eight hours of sleep or you'll collapse the next day?

"Pray without ceasing" — all day long, all night long. It's just a matter of having the communication system open between yourself and God so you can say at any time of day or night, "SOS, Lord." And He can say to you, "Knock, knock. There's a need down there. Will you please pray?"

> *Dear Father, I want to be available to You, twenty-four hours a day. Teach me to open my communication with You and never shut it.*

WRONG MOTIVES

When you ask, you do not receive, because you ask
with wrong motives, that you may spend what
you get on your pleasures.

James 4:3

The reason God sometimes answers no to our prayers is that we prayed with the *wrong* motives. Although the things for which we ask may be good in themselves, we want them for the wrong reasons. So, even though we do ask, we do not receive.

Motives are the *reasons* for praying as we do. The reason for praying for a certain thing can itself make it a "wrong prayer." What are wrong prayers? Those prayed to *"consume them upon Your lusts"* (James 4:3, KJV).

The word *lusts* in James 4:3 has been translated more recently as *pleasures,* and accurately so. But to us today, the word *pleasures* basically means something that is good and positive. Then there are things that are good for Christians that also are translated *pleasures* in the Bible. However, this particular biblical word *pleasures* always is negative and off-limits for Christians. The literal definition of the Greek word translated *pleasures* in James 4:3 is,

"The gratification of natural desire or sinful desires." This word is much better understood today when translated *lusts.*

The word, of course, is much broader in meaning than just sexual lusts. How shocking to realize that the prayers we ourselves are praying frequently are prayed with a wrong motive — to consume upon our lusts. And God must answer, "You prayed the wrong prayer."

Here are some of the common, everyday motives that creep into our praying: praise, fame, love of power, love of display, love of preeminence, status over others, ease, comfort, personal satisfaction, self-pleasing, self-vindication, gratification of sinful desires, and revenge.

While most of us are basically careful to pray for things we believe are good and which God wants to grant us, we usually are completely unaware of the wrong motives that can be inspiring in these prayers. And praying with wrong motives for things to which God usually answer yes spells failure in prayer.

➤ *Dear Father, Help me to examine my motives when I come before You in prayer.*

To Whom We Pray

Resist the devil and he will flee from you.
Draw near to God, and He will draw near to you.
James 4:7-8

An often overlooked but very important part of prayer is the drawing near to God. Before we are ready to start our intercessory prayers, we need to *wait* before God until we know we have established communication with Him. This is a time of silence when we are shutting out every other thought and distraction around us. This is not talking to God, just a complete mental drawing near to Him; and then, as He promised, *He will draw near to us.*

Drawing apart to God is important in groups as well as in private praying. It may be easier to do in our closets; but because of the hectic rush to arrive at a prayer meeting on time or because of the chatting after we've arrived, it is a must to pause for the seconds or minutes it takes to withdraw from all this and draw near to God. Often there seems to be embarrassment in a group if someone doesn't start praying audibly right away as we go to prayer — ready or not.

I remember struggling and struggling to draw

near to God. I can recall how I would strain and wonder where He was. And it seemed as if my prayers were only reaching the ceiling. But through the years God has taught me many things — and I'm not in the struggling stage any more.

One thing I learned when I found it impossible to establish meaningful communication with God was that it wasn't His fault; it was mine. He is the same yesterday, today, and forever, but I am not. I let sins creep in that break my fellowship with Him, and frequently I must search my heart and confess those sins that are blocking communication between us.

I also learned the simple process of envisioning my God when approaching Him in prayer. The joy that floods my whole being as I find myself visualizing all God is — all His holiness, all His love, all His power, all His concern for me — defies description. What greater privilege could there be for a human being than to actually *draw* near to the omnipotent, omniscient God, high and lifted up on His throne in glory? This to me is the most precious part of my prayer time.

➤ *O God, Thank You for the indescribable experience of drawing into Your presence. Give me the patience and discipline I need to draw near to You.*

Praying in Spiritual Warfare

Finally, be strong in the Lord and in His mighty power.
Put on the full armor of God so that you can take
your stand against the devil's schemes.
Ephesians 6:10-11

Ephesians 6:10-20 teaches there are two kinds of spiritual warfare praying—defensive (verse 18) and offensive (verses 19 and 20). Just as there are defensive and offensive tactics in sports, so are there in the spiritual battle.

In *defensive* tactics, the players try to defend and protect themselves and their goal line from the on-slaught of the opposing team rushing offensively against them. Likewise, in defensive praying the Christians pray for each other for protection in our mutual spiritual battle against Satan.

But *offensive* tactics are just the opposite of de-fensive. There the players rush against the oppos-ing team to score points. It is the same in offensive spiritual warfare praying. There the Christians in-vade Satan's territory "to score" by releasing those captive in his kingdom.

If there are only *defensive* plays in sports, the score would remain at a 0 to 0 tie, and nobody would win. To win in sports there must be offensive plays. And so it is in the spiritual battle for souls. There must be *offensive* plays—and prayers—if we are to rescue the lost from Satan's kingdom.

In that Ephesians 6 description of the spiritual battle, why did Paul tell Christians to put on God's armor? *Only* so they could stand firm against the devil's schemes?

Only so they could be safe from Satan's fiery darts? *Only* so they could stand—still? No. Paul concludes the armor portion with Christians actively *doing* something—*counterattacking Satan* with the Sword of the Spirit, the Word of God—and *praying.*

> *Lord, Help me to remember to "put on my armor" each day so that I can defend myself against spiritual attacks. Give me the courage to be strong in my prayer counterattack against Satan.*

OUR RESPONSE TO
GOD'S ANSWERS

*The jailer woke up, and when he saw the prison doors
open, he drew his sword and was about to kill himself
because he thought the prisoners had escaped. But
Paul shouted, "Don't harm yourself! We are all here!"*
Acts 16:27-28

People respond in various ways to God's answers to their prayers. Many different responses to prayer are recorded in the New Testament. There is the choice of *witnessing*. Anna prayed for many years to see the Messiah, and when God answered her prayers at Baby Jesus' circumcision, she went out and told everyone she had seen the Messiah. But Simeon's response was quite different. After praying the same prayer for a similar time period, he too saw the Messiah. His response? "Now I am ready to die."

There is the reaction of *disbelief*. As the early Christians prayed for Peter's release from prison, they could not believe that God had answered their prayers, thinking it was his ghost knocking at the gate. There is the response of *obedience*. Peter's prayers on the rooftop were answered by God in a vision he did not understand at the time. But even so, when God did explain it, Peter obeyed immediately and brought the Gospel to the Gentiles.

We have to make a *choice*. Paul and Silas prayed and sang in the prison, and God answered by sending an earthquake that opened all the doors and broke the prisoners' chains. But Paul chose to forego immediate freedom in order to win the jailer to Christ. Perhaps one of the most difficult responses to God's answer to prayer was Paul's response of *acceptance*. Paul prayed three times for his thorn in the flesh to be removed, but accepted God's answer, a "no" answer, relying at last on God's strength.

The Bible reveals myriads of different responses to God when He answered prayer — some good, some bad, some rebellious, some submissive, some joyous, some thankful, some angry. Our responses to God's answers to our prayers can be many and varied also. The decision is up to us.

➤ *Father, I want to glorify You in the way I respond to Your answers to my prayers. Help me not only to accept but to be joyful in all Your answers to my prayers.*

FOR WHOSE GLORY?

Since, then, you have been raised with Christ,
set your hearts on things above, where Christ is seated
at the right hand of God. Set your minds on things above,
not on earthly things.
Colossians 3:1-2

Wanting something for our own glory, not God's, is one reason why a prayer, although scripturally accurate and acceptable to God, is ruined by our reason for praying it.

Some years ago, as I prayed my birthday prayer for the coming year, my words simply were these: "God, You be glorified, not me!" And when the year ended, my praying for only His glory did not end. Praying the "right prayer" about God getting all the glory has been a learning process for me for a long time.

Through the years, I have prayed before speaking that I will not be seen as I speak—only Jesus. After the sometimes flowery introduction is all over, I pray that what I am wearing, my hairstyle, and so on will all fade from the audience's consciousness and be replaced by Jesus. The greatest compliment I ever receive is when someone steps up to me and quietly says, "I saw Jesus standing there instead of you all day today." For *His* glory!

Also, before a seminar, I always pray, "Lord, remove every illustration and point that will bring glory to me instead of You." The illustration or point may be very good in itself, but if my motive for bringing it is for *my* glory, God will not use it to move in the lives of those in my audience. It has to be for *His* glory.

We can even have the wrong motive in praying to win others to Christ. For whose glory do we want to bear spiritual fruit? Jesus in John 15:7-8 tells us that if we fulfill His conditions, we shall ask what we will and it shall be done unto us. But why? So that we can be glorified? Oh, no. It is so that we can bear much fruit—not for our glory but for the Father's. Are we trying to win another to Jesus to get credit ourselves? For whose glory?

A subtle motive of our receiving the glory instead of God slips in when we have discovered something exciting and shared it with someone, only to have that person come out with it later in a discussion, in a sermon, or in a book! How it hurts when another gets the credit instead of us. But then we must examine the reason for feeling this way. God can get a lot done if we don't care who gets the credit—and the glory!

➤ *Dear Father, I want You to get all the glory for every single thing You do through me. Please take all the glory. You, and You alone, deserve it.*

I AM NOT ABLE

*Now to Him that is able to do immeasurably more
than all we ask or imagine, according to His power
that is at work within us.*
Ephesians 3:20

After spending much time in deep intercessory prayer one morning, I asked God to bring to my mind the Scripture He had for me for that day's seminar. Ephesians 3:20 instantly flashed across my mind. But as I repeated the verse over and over, only two words kept standing out: *according to, according to.* I puzzled over what God was trying to teach me. The verse suddenly seemed so complicated; I decided to break it down. I lumped the words "immeasurably more than all we ask or imagine" into a simple "all that." God can do "all that." Then it read, "Now to Him that is able to do . . . all that . . . according to His power that is at work within us." I had it! God is able to do "all that" *only* according to the power that works in us!

Then I really began to ponder this in my heart. I asked myself, "Don't I have God's power in me all the time?" I must have, for as a Christian, all three persons of the Trinity dwell in me. I have Christ in me, "the hope of glory" (Colossians 1:27); the Father will come and dwell in us (1 John 4:12-15); and Jesus promised that the Holy Spirit would be in us (John 14:17). In fact, just before Paul's doxology in Ephesians 3, which includes verse 20, he prayed that the Christian at Ephesus would "be filled to the measure of all the fullness of God" (Ephesians 3:19).

The next question loomed, But do I always have the same amount of God's power working in me? From years of experience, I knew automatically that the answer was no. I do not have the same proportion of God's power all of the time. And He is able to do only in accordance with, in proportion to, the measure of the power which is working in me!

> *Dear Father, Fill me with Your transforming power so that Your work in my life can be accomplished.*

WE LIMIT GOD

*My message and my preaching were not with wise and
persuasive words, but with a demonstration of
the Spirit's power.*
1 Corinthians 2:4

What is it that releases greater amounts of God's power? Our prayers, of course! God sends His power in response to adequate praying.

God, through His answers, accomplishes what He has wanted to do all along but has been hindered by our lack of prayer. And although He is sovereign and can and does do as He chooses without the help of believers' prayers, He has chosen to operate extensively in response to them.

People frequently ask me how much time they should spend in personal closet praying. I reply, "That depends on how much power you want." E.M. Bounds in his book *Power through Prayer* explained, "Our short prayers owe their point and efficiency to the long ones that have preceded them. The short, prevailing prayer cannot be prayed by one who has not prevailed with God in a mightier struggle of long continuance." So, even though God can do anything He wants, He has chosen to permit us to limit many of His actions by our lack of faithfulness in prayer. Conversely, our sufficient praying will enable Him to give the answers we both desire.

God, with all the power of the universe, is sitting on His throne in glory, even today, waiting and longing to release that power on Planet Earth. With absolute unlimited power at His disposal (in fact, He *is* unlimited power), He is ready to pull aside the curtain and let us step into a new era of that power in our lives — appropriated by and released through prayer!

Since I found Jesus Christ personally at age nine, I've diligently prayed for others and myself. And I have depended on God's power through prayer in my whole life of ministry. What I have felt all of these years was summed up in January 1982, when I wrote in the margin of my Bible beside 1 Corinthians 2:4, "This is what I want for my ministry: 'My message and my preaching were not with wise and persuasive words, but with a demonstration of the Spirit's power.' " God has been faithful in sending that power in answer to the prayers of thousands of faithful pray-ers.

➤ *Lord, Give me the diligence to devote*
an adequate amount of time to You in prayer so that
all I do and say will be full to overflowing with Your power.

Praying for Souls

*They overcame him by the blood of the Lamb
and by the word of their testimony;
they did not love their lives so much
as to shrink from death.*
Revelation 12:11

S atan tries to fool people into thinking they are real Christians—especially Bible-studying members of fine churches—when they are not. Jesus said, "Not everyone who says to Me, 'Lord, Lord,' will enter the kingdom of heaven." Even to those who prophesied in His name, cast out demons, and in His name performed many miracles Jesus will say, "I never knew you. Away from me, you evildoers!" (Matthew 7:21-23)

Many years ago I learned a simple procedure that produces amazing results when giving an invitation to accept Jesus—or making sure He is Savior and Lord. Even though most of my seminar participants around the world belong to a church, I've learned not to assume they are all real Christians. So just before I give an invitation to accept Christ, I confront Satan directly about his deceiving them.

While the participants are praying in their small groups, I take the opportunity to pan the whole audience, looking briefly at each person in the room. Then I silently address him with, *"Satan, you have deceived these people long enough. Jesus died for every person in this room, and you have no right to deceive them, Satan. I am claiming the blood and the name of Jesus against you. I command you to leave, because you cannot stand against Jesus' name and His blood!"* (See Revelation 12:9-11.)

Then I turn to the Lord in prayer, asking Him to please save them—every one. Continuing to look over the audience, there is a deep aching in my heart for those dear ones sitting out there, lost. My praying for them feels like when I travailed in birth for my babies—struggling, longing for their birth. Re-birth in Jesus! "Father," I cry, "woo them, draw them, open their hearts to Jesus! Save them, please!"

➤ *O Lord, Penetrate the hearts of those who really don't know Jesus as their Savior. Defeat Satan, Father, so that they may experience Your wonderful salvation.*

In Our Midst

For where two or three come together in my name,
there am I with them.
Matthew 18:20

We must never underestimate the value of a small group praying, for Christ promised that *where two or three of His followers are gathered together in His name, He will be in their midst* (see Matthew 18:20). What an opportunity it provides to practice the presence of Christ in our midst!

Do you remember in the account of the stoning of Stephen that he lifted up his eyes and "saw the glory of God, and Jesus standing on the right hand of God"? (Acts 7:55) The right hand of God is the place of authority and honor. Christ is still at the right hand of God today, interceding for us, but we also have His promise that He will be with us — where even two or three are gathered together.

Now, we want to be very careful that we do not take Christ off His throne, that we do not play games with Him in prayer. He is in heaven, but His presence is in the midst of those who gather together in His name.

Christ helped the disciples and those who knew Him very intimately here on earth to understand this. G. Campbell Morgan, in his message "Rekindled Fire," emphasizes the importance of our Lord's vanishing and appearing after His resurrection. He explains that the disciples and His friends were learning the lesson that Christ was with them, even when they did not see Him with their physical eyes. These followers of Jesus were practicing His presence even though they could not see Him. After He had vanished from their sight for the last time at His ascension, He was in their midst in the Upper Room, and they knew it.

➢ *Dear Father, Please give me the privilege of being aware of the presence of Jesus, my Savior, in a prayer group. Teach my prayer group to wait expectantly for Jesus.*

In God's Will

*And this is the confidence which we have before Him,
that, if we ask anything according to His will, He hears us.*
1 John 5:14, NASB

Have you come to the place where you can pray, "Only God's will"? Do you know that you are in absolute oneness with the will of God? Have you come to that place?

We read in 1 John 5:14-15 about a prerequisite to effective praying. "And this is the confidence that we have in Him, that, if we ask anything according to His will, He hears us. And if we know that He hears us in whatever we ask, we know that we have the requests which we have asked from Him." Did you catch the prerequisite? How can we have confidence in anything we ask? By praying according to His will. And what is confidence in prayer? It is knowing absolutely and irrevocably that we have whatever we have asked.

What do we mean when we use the expression "praying in God's will"? Is it simply tacking on the end of a prayer the phrase we use perhaps more frequently than any other? You know how it goes. We ask God for a whole string of things, then we piously add, "If it be Thy will, Lord. Amen."

Praying in God's will is not easy, yet it's very simple. The secret is a commitment of every single thing that comes into our lives to God and His perfect will, until we no longer want anything that is not His will. And it's exciting to live in complete oneness with the will of God. It is never dull or static because it is not a one-time, once-for-all commitment. It is something we have to work at constantly, moment by moment. But the most exciting part is seeing God answer—when it is His will—and ours.

➤ *Lord, Help me to release my will to You*
in order to be able to pray according to Your perfect will.

Prayer Chain

"He will call upon me, and I will answer him;
I will be with him in trouble,
I will deliver him and honor him."
Psalm 91:15

One exceptional benefit of being in a telephone prayer chain is what it can do for your home. If you want to really teach prayer to your children, I know of no better way than prayer chain procedures.

As the children hear Mother calling through the prayer requests, and then watch as she bows her head immediately after putting down the receiver, they know that Mother believes in prayer. When the answer comes through they can hear her say, "Oh, that's great!" They watch her as she dials the next person on the prayer chain, and they listen as she says, "Praise God. He answered our prayer." They take note of her joy as she bows her head and thanks God for answering.

As prayer chain telephone calls come into the home, the children and other members of the family can observe the progress of prayer, taking note of specific requests, specific answers, God's timing, and the flow of praise.

For our family this has been one of the greatest teaching instruments through all the years of bringing up our children. They believe so much in prayer chains that both our daughters, when they were out of town, have spent their own money to call long distance with requests. Now our son, Kurt, the only child still living at home, every once in awhile comes out with, "I think it's time to call the prayer chain!"

Once while Kurt and I were painting the ceiling of our sun porch, the telephone rang, but I wasn't in any particular hurry to answer — I was up a ladder with the paint dripping down my arms! Our daughter Nancy picked up the kitchen phone, and in a few seconds she called in, "Never mind, Mother, it's *just* another answer to prayer."

Prayer chains provide a wonderful method of teaching complete confidence in answered prayer, and in the God who answers prayer. Let your children hear these specific answers that are reported over your telephone. It will do something for your entire family.

➤ *Lord, Thank You for the pray-ers in prayer chains and for the privilege of being one of them. And thank You for Your answers which teach us all so much.*

HAVE A THANKFUL HEART

And we pray this in order that you may live a life
worthy of the Lord and may please Him in every way:
bearing fruit in every good work, growing in the
knowledge of God, being strengthened with all power
according to His glorious might so that you may have
great endurance and patience, and joyfully giving
thanks to the Father, who has qualified you to
share in the inheritance of the saints
in the kingdom of light.
Colossians 1:10-12

What happens when God answers? The ultimate, final response on our part should be to thank Him. No matter how God has answered our prayer, the one thing He expects from us is thankfulness.

People tend to insert their thanksgiving at different places in the prayer process. Some never bother to thank God no matter how great and wonderful the answers He sends. Most people, but not all, are thankful when God answers the way they requested and has given them what they wanted. Then, some Christians have matured enough spiritually to thank Him in spite of how He has answered, trusting His divine wisdom.

But the Bible has an even greater requirement as to where the thanksgiving belongs in the whole prayer process. Philippians 4:6, surprisingly, reads, "Be anxious for nothing, but in everything by prayer and supplication *with thanksgiving* let your requests be made unto God" (NASB, emphasis mine).

It is rare indeed to find those who actually put their thanksgiving right in with the request. Few are able to be thankful *while* they are asking, because they are concentrating on the way they want God to answer. And the deeper the personal need or hurt, the more difficult it becomes to be thankful while begging God to intervene. Our minds usually are totally consumed by the problem, not with thanksgiving, during our wrestling in prayer. It takes deep maturity indeed to trust God enough to be able to thank Him before He answers, to be able to include the thanks *with* the request!

➤ *Lord, Thank You for Your overwhelming goodness to me. Give me the maturity to trust You completely so that I can thank You in all things — while I ask.*

MEDITATION CAN
BE DANGEROUS

*For what do righteousness and wickedness
have in common? Or what fellowship can
light have with darkness?*
2 Corinthians 6:14

Putting yourself into a state of passivity is a very dangerous spiritual exercise, and one in which even true Christians are engaging. To open our minds and allow ourselves to be receptive to all the thoughts and suggestions which enter is a perilous business. We may think we are drawing near to God—but zing! There's Satan, and we are listening to *his* voice.

At a prayer seminar, a woman stepped up to me and said, "Do you know that I taught yoga and gave it up?"

I said, "Tell me, why did you give it up?"

"Well," she replied, "I suddenly realized that there I was in that room meditating with Buddhists, with Hindus, with people involved in every religion you can imagine. Sure, you sit there and you meditate and you get a feeling of peace and strength; but I've learned that I get all the peace and strength I need from the Lord Jesus Christ, and I don't need yoga meditation. And God told me it's a sin for me to be meditating with those who do not know the true God in heaven."

Oh, how foolish to put ourselves in such a vulnerable position! It does make a difference with whom we attempt to draw near to God. "What do righteousness and wickedness have in common?" (2 Corinthians 6:14)

> ➤ *Lord, I want to always be on the alert for spiritual attack. Give me discernment and guide me to the wisdom found in Your Word.*

GETTING RID OF GRUDGES

*. . . when you stand praying, if you hold
anything against anyone, forgive him, so that your Father
in heaven may forgive you your sins.*
Mark 11:25

A man who attended one of my prayer seminars had loaned a relative $70, even though he could hardly spare the money. He shared his feelings with me after our session on forgiving others. "Evelyn," he said, "I just told God that I now forgive the one who borrowed that money a couple of years ago and has not even mentioned it to me since. I was becoming more and more bitter in my heart, and I now know that I have to go and confirm my love to that relative. So, after I get home tonight, I'm going to dig out that little promissory note for the $70 and write on it 'Paid in full,' and put it right in the mail."

For you to do:

1. Ask God to bring to your mind that person who has grieved you and whom you have not forgiven.

2. Ask God to forgive you for the sin of not forgiving that person.

3. Now forgive that person, asking God to give

you the strength and ability if you need to.

4. Now ask God for as much love as He wants you to have for the person who grieved you.

5. Next ask God how you should confirm your love to that person.

6. Wait in silence for His answer.

7. Pray, promising God that you will do whatever He has told you.

8. Go do it!

➤ *Lord, Help me to be obedient in Your command to forgive others.*

Satan and the Gospel Seed

"A farmer went out to sow his seed.
As he was scattering the seed,
some fell along the path; it was trampled on,
and the birds of the air ate it up."

Luke 8:5

In the parable of the sower Jesus gave us one of the reasons the Gospel seed doesn't bring forth fruit in unbelievers. He said some seed fell beside the path, and it was trampled underfoot, and the birds of the air ate it up (Luke 8:5). Then, explaining the parable to His disciples, Jesus said:

The seed is the Word of God. Those along the path are the ones who heard, and then the *devil* comes and takes away the Word from their hearts, so that they cannot believe and be saved (Luke 8:11-12, emphasis added).

Satan knows the power of God's Word. He knows people are "born again, not of perishable seed, but of imperishable, through the living and enduring Word of God" (1 Peter 1:23). One of his main tactics in keeping people in his kingdom is to snatch that Word before it takes root in their hearts.

In other words, when we share, preach, or teach the Word of God, Satan is right there snatching up that seed. And our efforts have been in vain. Nothing happens because the seed of the Gospel did not take root.

But Satan only can do this if the soil is hardened—like that along the path in Jesus' parable. So, how do we solve that problem of these hardened hearts? We pray!

We must *precede* the sowing of the seed with intense prayer. We need to pray specifically that God will go ahead of the seed and prepare the hearts of those who will hear. Pray for them individually, by name if possible—for their hearts to be softened. Then when the Word of God comes, that seed can take root instead of being gobbled up by Satan. And those we are trying to reach for Jesus will be saved.

Lord, I pray that _____'s heart would be softened,
so that Your Word will take root when it is planted.
Protect _____ from the tactics of Satan, and help
_____ to receive the Word and accept Jesus
as Savior and Lord.

HOLINESS

Make every effort to live in peace with all
and to be holy; without holiness
no one will see the Lord.
Hebrews 12:14

I f we expect God to answer our prayers, we must meet His requirement of holiness. The Triune God expects this of us. God the Father commands, "Be holy, because I am holy" (1 Peter 1:16). Paul writes in Romans 8:29 that we are "predestined to be conformed to the likeness of His Son"—Jesus, who, although tempted in all things as we are, was without sin (Hebrews 4:15). Then, "be filled with the [Holy] Spirit" (Ephesians 5:18). Holiness is the fundamental attribute of God and His requirement for us.

At one seminar, as I suggested we all read Galatians 5 and 6 until God spoke to each of us, I prayed, "O God, give me something very personal—just for me today." And He directed my eyes across the page to Ephesians, chapter 1. There it was—His word for me. "He chose us in Him before the creation of the world to be holy and blameless in His sight" (1:4). His requirement for me! Yes, holiness. Anything less in my life is sin. And "if I had cherished sin in my heart, the Lord would not have listened" (Psalm 66:18). So, here is the reason for many of God's seemingly negative answers.

"Is it all hopeless?" you ask. Oh, no! Continuously identifying and confessing our sins does produce the holy life that is necessary for God to hear and answer our prayers.

➤ *Dear Father, Cleanse me of every known sin so that I may be holy in Your sight — eligible to have You hear and answer my prayers.*

Repent

Therefore do not let sin reign in your mortal body
that you obey its evil desires. Do not offer the parts
of your body to sin, as instruments of wickedness,
but rather offer yourselves to God, as those who have
been brought from death to life; and offer the parts
of your body to Him as instruments of righteousness.
Romans 6:12-13

When we pray, "Father, I have sinned," how does God answer us? Does He say, "Now that you have confessed the fact that you have sinned, it will be all right"? Oh, no. God then commands us to "Repent!"

A bewildered wife called me asking for prayer. She said that her husband was sleeping with another woman, then getting up the next morning and asking God to forgive him. He told his wife it was OK because God always forgives us when we ask Him to. "Is this true?" the wife questioned. "Does he have a right as a Christian to live this way?"

"No," I replied, and then shared a part of Romans 6 with her: "Shall we go on sinning so that grace may increase? By no means!" (verses 1-2) "Therefore do not let sin reign in your mortal body that you obey its evil desires. Do not offer the parts of your body to sin, as instruments of wickedness, but rather offer yourselves to God, as those who have been brought from death to life; and offer the parts of your body to Him as instruments of righteousness" (verses 12-13).

After we have identified a specific action in our lives as sin and have admitted it to God in prayer, we humans are prone to say to ourselves, "Now, just forget it," or "Oh, that's really not a sin." Or we may say, "You really didn't mean to hurt anybody," or "That's not such a bad sin." But God says, "Repent!"

When we have admitted a sin, God never says, "Oh, that's all right, My child. Let's just forget it now, and you get on with your life." Oh, no. He doesn't say, "That's that," and close the curtain on the whole thing. He expects continued action on both our part and His. Our part is to repent.

➤ *O Lord, I repent of all my sins.*
Thank You for Your perfect forgiveness.

THE PROUD PRAY-ER

. . . when you pray, do not be like the hypocrites,
for they love to pray standing in the synagogues
and on the street corners to be seen by men.
I tell you the truth, they have received their reward in full.
Matthew 6:5

Many of our prayers are prayed with wrong motives. One wrong motive is *to be seen by people,* not God—so we will get the credit and glory. But Jesus, in Matthew 6:5, said our motive for praying is not to be as that of the hypocrites standing in the synagogues and on the street corners in order "to be seen by men." This is a wrong motive; no matter how good the content of these prayers might be, the Lord is displeased.

This is the lust of display—one of the major reasons we ask and have not. How proud we can become by being known as "one who never skips a prayer meeting" or "one who prays such beautiful prayers in public." Things good in themselves but done with the wrong motive. The lust of pride! God told Solomon that it was only when His people would *"humble themselves* and pray" that He would answer and "heal their land" (2 Chronicles 7:14, emphasis mine).

There also can be the motive of pride in our private devotional praying. I find that I must be constantly on the alert for wrong motives in my own prayer life, and usually, I am surprised when they surface.

In the whole section of James 4:1-3, one of the reasons for not receiving is that "you are envious" (verse 2, NASB). We always want immediate success, victory, and credit when praying for someone we love, but our motives can be to consume it upon our lust — our pride.

James 4:6 tells us that "God opposes the proud," so He certainly won't grant our requests that are prayed because of our lust or pride. A wrong motive makes it a wrong prayer — which, of course, God won't answer.

> ➤ *Lord, Examine my motives. Open my eyes*
> *so I can see when my motives in prayer*
> *are more prideful than pure.*

YOUR KINGDOM, NOT MINE

*"Our Father in heaven, hallowed be Your name,
Your kingdom come, Your will be done on earth
as it is in heaven."*
Matthew 6:9-10

How many Christian leaders are building their own kingdoms, not God's? Here again, what they are praying for may be good and scriptural — a growing congregation, a larger church building, better headquarters for their organization or campus — but their *reason* for praying is for praise, fame, and glory for themselves.

But Jesus in His model prayer in Matthew 6, as He taught His followers to pray, was very explicit about whose kingdom must be built: "Our Father . . . *Your* kingdom come . . . on earth as it is in heaven" (verses 9-10, emphasis mine).

In a large, seemingly successful church in which I held a seminar, several members commented sadly to me, "But there is no power." Why? Perhaps it was because their very talented pastor might have been building not the kingdom of God and His glory but his own kingdom and his own reputation.

This love of preeminence, status over others, and building one's own kingdom instead of God's seemed already to be a problem in the first century. In 3 John, the Apostle John said that he needed to expose Diotrephes because he loved to be first among people and refused to acknowledge John, lest his own position of authority should be challenged.

We tend to think this wrong motive exists only in the large, splashy ministries; however, it may be as true or even more true in the small, struggling churches and organizations. In a desperate attempt to prove their importance, such churches may resort to building their own kingdom instead of God's.

It is possible that we are deceiving ourselves, as well as other people, about our motives in prayer — but never God. He is aware of all our hidden attitudes and motives — many times unrecognized even by ourselves.

It is not only our words that ascend to God in prayer but our motives as well. God looks within — and our motives are just as obvious to Him as our spoken words. "Then all the churches will know that I am He who searches the hearts and minds" (Revelation 2:23).

Praying with the wrong motive, then, is praying anything to which God must answer "no" because, although perhaps good in itself, the reason for praying is "to spend what you get on your pleasures [of pride]" (James 4:3).

➤ *Dear Father, Please search my heart for my wrong motives in even the good things I pray for. Cleanse me, O God, and keep me always building Your kingdom, not mine.*

MOTIVATION IN PRAYER

If anyone turns a deaf ear to the law,
even his prayers are detestable.

Proverbs 28:9

Praying with wrong motives is actually the cause of praying the wrong prayers.

We like to think that the "you ask with wrong motives" of James 4:3 is just slightly missing the right content in our prayer. However, it means wicked, evil asking. To ask with wrong motives means: "to ask evilly." It is praying for the satisfaction of those things that God explicitly calls on the true Christian to suppress. Thus, it is not a prayer that can be answered by God. A prayer prayed with the wrong motive must be answered by Him, "You prayed the wrong prayer."

But in John 15:7, didn't Jesus promise that we could ask for *"whatever* [we] wish"? And then in this chapter's sixteenth verse, didn't He say that "the Father will give you whatever you ask in My name"? How, then, could anything we pray for be asking with wrong motives and a "wrong prayer"?

Well, Jesus also gave us innumerable rules by which to live; and His promise for answers to our prayers did not, and could not, negate all His rules and commands. Jesus is truth (John 14:6). He cannot lie. Could He teach and demand purity, holiness, and righteousness and then imply in His prayer promises that we could ask for—and receive—just the opposite?

Again, Jesus said in John 14:14, "If you ask Me *anything* in My name, I will do it" (NASB, emphasis mine)—seemingly giving us a blank check to request any amount of anything we choose. However, in His preceding words, He clearly says *why* He will do whatever we ask in His name—"that the Father may be glorified in the Son" (John 14:13, NASB). So, obviously, Jesus would never promise anything in answer to prayer that would not glorify the Father. And certainly, those things that God calls on us to suppress because they are sin would not be granted—even if prayed "in the name of Jesus."

No—all of our prayers must conform to and adhere to God's rules and laws as set forth for us in the Bible. They must be based on scriptural guidelines. They must be in the confines of God's will as set forth in Scripture. Proverbs 28:9 actually says, "He that turneth away his ear from hearing the law [literally the Word of God], *even his prayer shall be abomination*" (KJV, emphasis mine).

➤ *Dear Father, Show me the wrong prayers*
I have been praying. Please forgive me for not reading
the Bible enough to find Your right things
for which I ought to pray.

RESPONSES

Look to the Lord and His strength; seek His face always.
1 Chronicles 16:11

I t is awesome to realize that at the end of our lives we will be the sum total of our responses to God's answers to our prayers, for God has chosen to be limited in His next action by our response to His previous answer.

The final outcome of our lives is decided by a life-long series of responses to God's answers to our prayers. The way we respond to God and then He, in turn, to us actually determines the direction our lives will take.

It would be wonderful if each response to God affected only our lives at that point and no more. But not so. One response triggers the domino principle that affects all the rest of life. A major wrong response slips or hurtles us into the path of lost opportunities and missed spiritual growth, limiting God from taking us down the path He intended and planned for us.

As I grow older, it is interesting to look back on what seemed to be my correct responses and wonder "what if" I had not followed God's leading in that initial word from Him. What if I had not obeyed His initial call of "See, I have placed before you an open door" (Revelation 3:8), when I sought His face about the original prayer experiment that produced my prayer ministry? What path would I have taken? How far astray might I have gone before He would have given me another chance to respond correctly?

We really do determine our own spiritual growth rate, usefulness to God, and new opportunities by the way we respond to Him. At any point, we can hinder or stop His plan for our lives by our rebellious response to Him. Only in eternity will we see "what might have been" had our responses not thwarted God's plans for us. But with each step of obedience to God's answer to our prayers, He holds us gently yet firmly in that perfect path He has for us—walking hand in hand with Him.

➤ *Lord, I want to respond to You in obedience. Please give me the wisdom to follow Your path.*

Restore That Sinner

*Brothers, if someone is caught in a sin,
you who are spiritual should restore him gently.*
Galatians 6:1

When catching a sister or brother sinning, how often we pray, "Oh, God, what do I do now?" And the surprising answer from God is already recorded in the Bible. "Restore that sinner!"

What does it mean to restore? Paul had in mind here the mending of something that had been damaged. Restoration is the responsibility of those Christians surrounding the sinner. Repentance, reconciliation, and restitution are all the responsibility of the sinner; but, shockingly, restoration very likely must be done by the one sinned against, and it may even be the victim's job.

However, restoration does not begin while the person is sinning. It is when he or she is "caught" trespassing that the process begins. There can be no real restoration without the sinner fulfilling the other three "R's" preceding it — repentance, reconciliation, and restitution. Paul leaves no excuse in his teaching for Christians who are sinning, but makes it clear that the person who has sinned can be restored. But it is only the sinner whom God has accepted back through His forgiveness that we should accept back and restore.

This seems to be a lost teaching in recent years. We have been handling the sinning brother or sister one of two ways. Either we have ignored the sin, finding it much more comfortable not to become involved, or we have followed the scriptural injunction to rebuke him but with no further concern for the repentant one's well-being and restoration.

Although sin is not to be tolerated, there are definite steps the Christian church must take when a brother or sister sins. And the final step in this whole process is restoring the sinner to fellowship and ministry.

Jesus told His followers in Luke 17:3, "So watch yourselves. If your brother sins, rebuke him, and *if he repents,* forgive him" (emphasis mine). It is when the sinner repents that Christian action begins.

➤ *Father, Teach me Your steps in the restoration process. Help me to examine where I am in all my relationships with others and help me to be a restorer to those who have sinned.*

GOD'S INCREDIBLE PROVISION

Therefore, since we have been justified through faith,
we have peace with God through our Lord Jesus Christ.
Romans 5:1

While God's holiness demands reconciliation by a sacrifice for our sin, His love provided it!

God loved us enough to send the means of reconciliation—His own Son, Jesus. Romans 5:8 says, "But God demonstrates His own love toward us in this: While we were yet sinners, Christ died for us." Jesus was the sacrifice that satisfied the demands of God's violated holiness. And this—God's own love—has saved us from His own wrath.

Christ came not only to preach the Gospel but so that there would be a Gospel to be preached! "God made Him who had no sin to be sin for us, so that in Him we might become the righteousness of God" (2 Corinthians 5:21). Overwhelmed, my heart cries, "How could He not spare His own Son but deliver Him up for us, and do it while we were still His enemies?"

Reconciliation is the removal of God's wrath toward man by the shedding of Jesus' blood on the cross. Through Jesus, our status with God is changed. We stand in the presence of the Holy God of heaven, justified—just as if we never had sinned, and reconciled—with God's wrath toward us eradicated, erased. "Not counting men's sins against them" (2 Corinthians 5:19). Reconciled!

Charles Colson, in a college commencement address, put it this way: "The Gospel of Jesus Christ must be the bad news of the conviction of sin before it can be the Good News of redemption."

In May of 1983, while on my way to a British Broadcasting interview, my taxi was following a bus with a sign on the back that read, "Therefore, since we have been justified through faith, we have peace with God through our Lord Jesus Christ" (Romans 5:1). After looking at it for many minutes, I suddenly realized the importance of the preposition "with." When we are justified at salvation, we don't receive the peace *of* God but peace *with* God.

Are you sure that you have been reconciled to God by accepting Jesus as your Savior and Lord? If not, have you ever considered that God is angry since you are still living in the state of sin into which you were born? And that He is angry because you are violating His holiness? But—have you also considered that He loves you so much that He is just waiting and longing to change His relationship with You? Be reconciled to God!

➤ *O God, Thank You for providing a*
perfect sacrifice for my sin! I want to make sure
today that I have been forgiven and reconciled
to You through accepting Jesus.

"I Don't Want To"

Make sure that nobody pays back wrong for wrong,
but always try to be kind to each other
and to everyone else.
1 Thessalonians 5:15

After someone has sinned against us, there may be the possibility that we don't want that sinner restored. We may prefer to say, "Good, you got what was coming to you. Squirm in the results of your sin! Retaliation is what you will get from me, not restoration!" But restoration, not retaliation or retribution, is God's New Testament command to us. "See that no one repays another with evil for evil, but always seek after that which is good for one another and for all men" (1 Thessalonians 5:15, NASB). Then again in Romans 12:17, "Do not repay anyone evil for evil."

There are many reasons why we knowingly or subconsciously really do not want the sinner to be restored. As long as they are not restored, we appear so much more spiritual in contrast to them. We, the victims, get so much more sympathy for the burden we are carrying if they remain in their sinning state. And people may even compliment us on what a great job we are doing holding them up.

Or, perhaps we need the sinner to keep depending on us. We need to be the strong, victorious, forgiving leader. It helps our own self-image when they are groveling at our feet in remorse, shame, and defeat.

I was surprised at the warning to me included in Galatians 6:1, "But watch yourself, or *you may also be tempted*" (emphasis mine). Reading verse 3, I cried, "O God, forgive me for thinking I'm better than the one I'm restoring. Search my heart lest I be tempted too—before I am."

Then, of course, there is the possibility of our being jealous of the repentant sinner being restored to a great ministry, feeling they have no right to achieve once more and perhaps even surpass us. But, no matter what our excuses, God says in His Word, *"Restore that sinner!"*

➤ *Dear Father, Make me a restorer to those who need me.*
Take my hurts from other people and in Your time,
and in Your way, restore me to perfect oneness
with them and to perfect rest in You.

"That Is Not for You"

In his heart a man plans his course,
but the LORD determines his steps.

Proverbs 16:9

At times we may pray for something good and even scriptural that God has decided is not for us. For other people perhaps—but not for us. Our persistence in this prayer does no good for this can be one of God's "you prayed the wrong prayer" answers.

While in my thirties, I prayed repeatedly for the "gift of administration," which, of course, is one of the gifts mentioned in 1 Corinthians 12:28 in the list of spiritual gifts. I had watched my husband's secretary with her tremendous gift of administration and longed for it too. I kept thinking of all the wonderful things I could organize for God—if He just would give me the gift of administration.

So I begged and pleaded with God to give me this gift. But this was the wrong prayer—God never gave me the gift of administration. However, it was not until I finally realized that God withholds gifts just as deliberately as He gives them that I understood He knew what He was doing, and I accepted His no answer.

But this was not God being mean and withholding a good scriptural gift. It was God answering me that He had called me "according to His purpose" and not according to what I thought I should be and do. God knew that I would have just twenty-four hours each day, and He had decided before the foundation of the world how He wanted me to spend them. I had been praying the wrong prayer.

I still occasionally wish I had that wonderful gift, but God's plan for me from the beginning was that I should study and teach, not spend time reorganizing everybody and everything.

So, praying for a gift God absolutely did not intend for me to have was spending all that time praying the wrong prayer. And through the years, He graciously has provided my Sally, whose gift *is* that wonderful gift of administration, to run my ministry while I do those things He *did* equip me to do.

➤ *Father, Give me the wisdom to pray for the things You have for me. And give me the grace to release to You those I think I should have.*

JESUS AND REPENTANCE

"The time has come," He said.
"The kingdom of God is near.
Repent and believe the good news."
Mark 1:15

W hen Jesus Christ, the Son of God, began His ministry on earth, He proclaimed the same message as John the Baptist had to prepare His way: "Repent!" He came into Galilee preaching, "The time has come," He said. "The kingdom of God is near. Repent and believe the good news!" (Mark 1:15)

Jesus, also, seeing sinful men in contrast to His Father's holiness and His own sinlessness, commanded them to repent throughout His earthly ministry. He was so disturbed by the sin He saw on earth that, in His Sermon on the Mount, He actually said it was better to cut off the offending member of our body than for the whole body to perish in hell (Matthew 5:29).

Then, after dying and paying the price for all sin, some of the final words the resurrected Jesus gave to His followers are recorded in Luke 24:46-47, where He admonishes them to keep on preaching repentance to all nations:

He told them, "This is what is written: The Christ should suffer and rise from the dead the third day, and repentance and forgiveness of sins will be preached in His name to all the nations, beginning at Jerusalem."

Then Peter, so fresh from his own repentance, immediately obeyed Jesus' command in his very first sermon, admonishing the nonbelieving men of Israel, "Repent, and be baptized, every one of you, in the name of Jesus Christ so that your sins may be forgiven" (Acts 2:38; see also Acts 3:18-19).

So the purpose of Jesus' coming, His preaching, and His death and resurrection was that repentance for forgiveness of sins could be proclaimed in His name to everyone, everywhere. And it is still His concern as He lives back in heaven with His Father.

Right now, Jesus is at the right hand of the Father interceding for us. For what is He praying? Only for our strength, power, grace, and guidance? I think not. For, since He had to send instructions (in Revelation 2 and 3) to the young churches to repent, what might He be praying for us today? Is He interceding for me, for you, for our churches—right now—that we will repent?

➤ *Lord God, I believe You have delivered me from my sins at salvation. I'm sorry for those I have committed as a Christian. Please forgive me as I turn from them.*

Forgive Yourself

You are kind and forgiving, O Lord,
abounding in love to all who call to You.
Psalm 86:5

The forgiven sinner must accept God's forgiveness. How often God cries, "I forgave you. Won't you please let Me open the curtain to that beautiful room called 'forgiven'?" A room filled with the sweet aroma of God's forgiveness. Its sweetness is surprisingly pleasant, not only to the nostrils but to the whole being. Saturating, engulfing, it completely obliterates any lingering stench of that sin. But the response is up to us.

A young woman who had had an abortion later married and tried for years to become pregnant. After exhaustive medical tests and experiments, the final conclusion was that pregnancy was impossible. In the depths of despair, she cried, "I killed the only baby I'll ever have!" How tragic to be unable to accept God's forgiveness when there had been deep repentance. How sad not to be able to walk once again with God in the cool of the garden — forgiven.

God cannot restore the sinner until that sinner accepts His forgiveness. My son-in-love, Skip, said this to me the other day, "After God has forgiven you and you have gone to your brother, if you can't forgive yourself, you are setting your standards higher than God's."

The greatest enemy of restoration may be ourselves. Complete restoration can come to the repentant sinner only when the self-loathing and the sometimes paranoid existence is exchanged for God's loving acceptance.

I sat listening to the widow of a prominent pastor who, after sinning grievously, had committed suicide. "When he repented deeply, the children and I forgave him, the church forgave him, God forgave him—but," she hung her head and sighed, "he could not forgive himself."

➢ *Lord, Thank You for the forgiveness You give when I have sinned and repented. Help me to accept Your forgiveness and forgive myself as well.*

WHO'S ANGRY?

The wrath of God is being revealed from heaven
against all the godlessness and wickedness of men
who suppress the truth by their wickedness.

Romans 1:18

Since reconciliation is necessary only when there is enmity and hostility between people or groups, we must ask, "Who's angry?" The surprising answer is "God!"

Why does God insist on reconciliation? Because He too is angry at our sinning.

The Bible never speaks of God being reconciled to man, only of people being reconciled to God. Although people are frequently angry with God, He never has to be reconciled to us because we are angry. God never sins or errs in His relationship with us, thus necessitating reconciliation back to us. Only we sin against Him.

God was so grieved and angry at sin that He was ready to blot out all the people on earth—with the exception of righteous Noah and his family (see Genesis 6:5-8). David too knew all about God's wrath when he cried in Psalm 6:1, "O Lord, do not rebuke me in Your anger or discipline me in Your wrath."

The same truth is carried over into New Testament teaching. John the Baptist, almost echoing Jesus' words to Nicodemus in John 3:18, explained to His disciples that "whoever believes in the Son has eternal life, but whoever rejects the Son will not see life, for God's wrath remains on him" (John 3:36).

Then after the death of Christ, Paul in Romans 1:18 warns, "The wrath of God is being revealed from heaven against all the godlessness and wickedness of men who suppress the truth by their wickedness."

I was at a dinner the night before a seminar where a fine young woman told me her story. Although she had been deeply into the drug scene, she had wanted cassette tapes of the Bible. Her hippie friends later chided her, saying, "What are you listening to *that* for?" And she, high on drugs, would giggle and say flippantly, "Oh, it's just the Bible!"

But one day while taking a drag on a joint of marijuana, she heard on the tape, "It is a fearful thing to fall into the hands of the living God" (Hebrews 10:31).

"Oh," she cried out in fright, "I don't want that to happen to me!" And she immediately accepted Christ.

➤ *O God, I confess that I have violated Your holiness*
and, thus, our relationship is broken. Please, God,
cleanse me from all known and unknown sin —
but be loving enough to forgive me and to
reconcile me to Yourself.

"My Will, Not Yours"

Do not be quick with your mouth,
do not be hasty in your heart
to utter anything before God.
God is in heaven and you are on earth,
so let your words be few.
Ecclesiates 5:2

Sometimes, we try to thwart God's will by the prayers we pray. But God then answers, "You are praying the wrong prayer." We must never forget that God is sovereign.

A pastor's wife told me that her husband was so enamored with his mistress (a woman in their church) that he always walked the long way to and from church just to walk by her house. Living in this sin and guilt, he was on the verge of an emotional collapse. But his wife told me she was trying to protect him from God's wrath and was continually praying: "O God, he's so close to a nervous breakdown—don't convict him of his sin. He won't be able to handle it. He'll collapse emotionally."

"What a desperately wrong prayer to pray," I told her. "The only hope for your husband is for God to show him that what he is doing is a grievous sin—and then to so convict him that he will repent, straighten out, and turn from his wicked ways."

God's will is never to coddle a sinner and just ignore the sin because we ask Him to. No, this is praying strictly against His will—and praying the wrong prayer.

We must be careful not to pray these wrong prayers, for the outcome may not be as great as we expected it to be. The Bible tells us that God sometimes will actually give us our request, but it will not be with His blessing, but with His judgment. When the Children of Israel left Egypt and journeyed to the Promised Land, Psalm 106:14-15 tells us that they "lusted exceedingly in the wilderness, and tempted God in the desert. And He gave them their request; but sent leanness into their soul" (KJV).

How can we be sure we are not "praying the wrong prayer"? First, we must stay in the Bible to become aware of what is right and what is wrong in God's eyes. This will enable us to identify those prayer requests that are innately evil in themselves. Then, after praying a request, we wait in God's presence, letting Him examine our motives for praying what we did. And God will bring these wrong motives to our minds and guard us from praying "wrong prayers."

> *Lord, Give me wisdom daily from*
Your Word so that when I am in prayer
I will pray according to Your will.

Delight in the Lord

*. . . I urge you, as aliens and strangers in the world,
to abstain from sinful desires, which war against your soul.*
1 Peter 2:11

A young wife and mother kept calling me from Hawaii about her husband and his girlfriend. One day, she asked, "Is it all right for me to ask God, if it is His will, to allow my husband to leave me and marry her, because God wants him to be happy?"

"No," I retorted, "don't ever pray that prayer. God's answer to that prayer already is in the Bible. God explicitly said that it is not His will for a marriage to break up." I explained to her that, in Matthew 19:6, God clearly said, "So they are no longer two, but one. Therefore what God has joined together, let man not separate." Then I told her God's words in Malachi 2:16 as He almost thundered, "I hate divorce." You do not pray for the fulfillment of your husband's sexual lusts—but for him to suppress them. Resentment and refusal to submit ourselves to any kind of scripturally required restraint is sin. And praying for things in opposition to what God's Word teaches certainly is "wrong praying."

Our bodies and minds are the camping ground

and battlefield of these lusts. So how could God grant us our wishes when those things for which we pray wage spiritual war within us? Praying for them is grossly "asking amiss."

The history of Christendom reveals many parallels of asking for God's blessing on something evil—slave traders piously asking God's blessing on their wicked traffic, and Italian outlaws propitiating their patron saint before attacking bands of travelers. Today, how many of us piously lift our voices to the holy God of heaven and then ask for something He calls an abomination?

God never promised, "Delight yourself in your neighbor's wife, and I will give you the desires of your heart." No! The psalmist told us God's way: "Delight yourself *in the Lord* and He will give you the desires of your heart" (Psalm 37:4, emphasis mine).

God rebukes us for delighting in the wrong thing. But Paul gives us an example of praying "the right prayer" in his prayer for those in the church at Thessalonica. "With this in mind, we constantly pray for you, that our God may count you worthy of His calling, and that by His power He may fulfill every good purpose of yours and every act prompted by your faith" (2 Thessalonians 1:11-12).

Every prayer, in order to be the "right prayer" which can be answered by God, must pass the test of His omniscience, His sovereignty, and His holiness.

➤ *Father, I know I am guilty of praying the wrong prayer at times. Please help me to delight myself in You, so that my prayers will be right and acceptable to You.*

Is the World Ready?

. . . pray in the Spirit on all occasions
with all kinds of prayers and requests.
With this in mind, be alert and always keep
on praying for the saints.
Ephesians 6:18

I n our impatience, we try to tell God when we want our prayers answered. But our good God controls the timing of His answers to our prayers. However, our prayers do start a process in our lives that prepares us for the answer — only to emerge years later as the answer to what we desired so long before.

It is also possible that God knows we are not ready for His answer — and the world may not yet be ready for what He has called us to do. For years before the printing of my book, *What Happens When Women Pray,* people at my prayer retreats and seminars would say that they thought the ideas about what produces power in prayer should be in print. "If you think so," I would always answer, "then you pray about it."

But when God did say, almost miraculously, "Write it!" I realized that something new was happening in our country. There was a turning of

Christians to a dependence on God not known for many years. We had been an "I can do it myself, God" generation. But Watergate had humbled us, and we became "the ugly Americans" in many places overseas. Christians were ready and eager to learn more about prayer. I believe that had the book been published sooner it would not have sold as many copies. But when it did come out, people were ready to pray. God's timing, not mine!

I have learned that God's timing is not my timing in the big and little things about which I pray. Sometimes God keeps me persisting in prayer, becoming more fervent in my wrestling with Him, through days, months, and even years. And then there are times when I know He is directing me to release the request back to Him after praying, and I just wait for His answer to come—when He decides it is time to send it.

But He always answers. In my life, there are what I call "answer times," which come suddenly—when God knows it is time, and multiple answers just start flowing. And I struggle to grasp them all, like feverishly plucking dandelion seeds scattering in the wind.

> ➤ *Lord, Thank You for Your perfect timing*
> *in answering my prayers. Teach me to trust*
> *You completely while I wait.*

A Prerecorded Answer

*All Scripture is God-breathed and is useful
for teaching, rebuking, correcting and training
in righteousness. . . .*

2 Timothy 3:16

God frequently answers our prayer inquiries with, "I already told you that." Then He adds, "I prerecorded that answer for you!" How? Where? In the Bible. God has prerecorded in His Holy Word most of the instructions we will ever need in our whole lifetime. Then He leads us to them in direct answer to our prayers.

This is an amazing procedure in which God does not give the answer during our prayer, as He frequently does, but rather leads us to the Scripture that contains the answer to our request. When we pray, asking Him for something specific, He replies with a specific prerecorded answer from the Bible.

Why can we get specific answers from a book whose closing words were written almost 2,000 years ago? Because the Bible is the only book on Planet Earth where the Author is always present while it is being read.

I am always surprised at people's reaction to having the actual author of a book in their midst. Some stand in awe, wondering if they might touch us, while others question if we are really human. Yet, the very God of the universe is present with us every time we read His book. But how few of us treat the Bible that way! How little awe or excitement we display at having its Author, the very God of heaven, actually speaking to us about our personal needs and desires. In fact, many people seem to ignore Him completely while reading and studying the Bible.

God communicates with us through the Bible in many different ways. While reading or studying His Word we may or may not know our need, but God does. And He takes the initiative to rebuke, comfort, or instruct us as we are reading. However, this method is different. Being acutely aware of a need or some instruction, we seek His answer in prayer, then God brings to our minds the place where He already has recorded the answer in the Bible.

➤ *Lord, Please make Your "prerecorded" answers obvious to me as You send me to Your Word, recorded before I even had the problem.*

WAITING

I waited patiently for the Lord;
He turned to me and heard my cry.
Psalm 40:1

One of the most difficult parts of obedience is waiting. It almost seems like seeing the flash of His lightning, and having only to wait and wait for the boom of the thunder of His power, accomplishing what He called us to do.

There are two kinds of waiting for answers to our prayers. First, there is the kind where we wait in His presence until He answers. We practice this in our prayer seminars while praying through the 2 Corinthians 2 forgiving formula. I ask all to pray aloud in their groups of four for God's love for the one they just forgave. Then I request that they wait—in silence—until they feel that love come. And it is amazing how we can feel God's love just descending on all of us—answering immediately, while we wait.

I do this same waiting personally in my daily devotions. Before each seminar or speaking engagement, I always pray, "Lord, fill me for today." And many times, the answer comes immediately with the warm, powerful filling for that day's ministry.

But it does not always come so quickly. Sometimes, even after exhausting all the requirements in my life that need to be prayed through, I finally pray, "Lord, I will not rise from my knees until You bless me! I will not even take time to eat breakfast before this huge day if You don't bless me!" Then I wait on my knees, often struggling in prayer, for His answer until it comes.

But there is a second kind of waiting for answers to our prayers in which we must give God more time to answer. We must pray and trust in His sovereignty while we wait for Him to answer — in His timing. But this waiting sometimes is spent persisting in prayer; and other times, God assures us that we have done our part and can release it to Him.

The Bible is full of accounts of those called by God who waited for Him to carry out their commitment. Moses' heart burned within him to rescue his people from their taskmasters in Egypt, but God sent him to the desert for forty years before consummating that call into action.

Even Jesus, after His resurrection, told His followers that they had to wait before they could bring this earth-shaking news to the world. So, after His ascension, they waited for ten whole days — in prayer. Waited for His Pentecost promise of power!

➤ *Dear Father, Give me the patience I need to wait for Your promises and the spiritual maturity to know unequivocally that You know best.*

TONES OF VOICE: 1

*. . . you must understand that no prophecy
of Scripture came about by the prophet's own interpretation.
For prophecy never had its origin in the will of man,
but men spoke from God as they were carried along
by the Holy Spirit.*
2 Peter 1:20-21

I can almost hear the different tones in God's voice when He gives us His "prerecorded" answers. He doesn't chant in the monotone with which we tend to read the Scripture. Sometimes, He uses a chiding tone with us for not remembering what He has already told us or a scolding tone when we ask, but already know His answer. Then sometimes, it seems as though He sighs in relief that we have finally asked. Here's an example of a response God could use in answering the questions we ask in our prayers.

"Don't insult Me," God declares in an indignant voice when we whine, "God, is it all right if I do so and so?" "Father, is it OK if I tell it this way? You know it's just a little white lie." "Could I have just a 'little friendly time' with him or her?" "Is it permissible for me to spend just this one little check without reporting it for taxes?"

Outraged, God answers, "If you have to ask *if,* you already know My answer. Don't insult Me by asking!"

Hebrews 1:1-2 tells us that God had communicated with us in two ways—through the prophets of long ago and then through the manifestation of His Son, Jesus. But since Jesus returned to heaven at His ascension, how does the Father now communicate with us? One way is by answering our prayers. A large percentage of answers to prayer were recorded by "holy men of God" (2 Peter 1:21, NASB) for us in the Bible.

So, let us not insult God by asking again when we already know what He has prerecorded for us. There are prayers we do not pray because He has already answered them in the Bible.

> ➤ *Dear Father, Teach me to use*
> *what You have already said in the Bible to answer*
> *my questions and solve my problems.*

Tones of Voice: 2

I urge that requests, prayers, intercession and thanksgiving be made for everyone — for kings and all those in authority, that we may live peaceful and quiet lives in all godliness and holiness. This is good, and pleases God our Savior, who wants all men to be saved and to come to a knowledge of the truth.

1 Timothy 2:1-4

God may impatiently answer our prayers with an, *"I already told you that,"* reminding us when He has prerecorded specific instructions about the matter we are questioning.

People frequently question me about asking God if it is His will that they pray for the salvation of another person. God must sigh patiently — or more likely, impatiently — at these prayers as He leads them once again to His prerecorded will in 2 Peter 3:9, telling them that He is not willing for *any* to perish. Or to 1 Timothy 2:1-4 where He tells us that praying for others is good and acceptable in His sight, because He desires all to be saved. So His prerecorded answer once again is "I already told you that."

But they also ask another question of God, "God, since it is Your will that none should perish, why don't You answer my prayer and make them accept Christ?" And God replies that He also has a law that He will not break—that every person has been given a free will. He will not allow any person to usurp the inalienable right of every human being—the right of free choice. Otherwise, Jesus would have declared that every inhabitant in Jerusalem had to be saved; but instead, He wept over them wanting to gather them as a hen gathers her chicks, but they were unwilling (Matthew 23:37).

"So the reason you should pray for them," God replies, "is that I will woo them and move in their lives in proportion to your prayers." It is not enough just to desire the salvation of the lost. Paul not only desired that the lost be saved but prayed to that end, "Brothers, my heart's desire and prayer to God for the Israelites is that *they* may be saved" (Romans 10:1, emphasis mine).

> ➤ *Father, Keep me persistent in my prayers for*
> *the unsaved, knowing that You will woo them as I pray.*

TONES OF VOICE: 3

. . . God has surely listened and heard my voice in prayer.
Psalm 66.19

I *knew you were going to hurt,"* God tenderly answers our anguished cry for help, "so I wrote these tender words of comfort to heal your broken heart."

"Let Me explain that," God calmly instructs my befuddled mind with His voice of omniscience. Then He directs me to His prerecorded answer that clears up the puzzle and enlightens my confused mind.

"Speak with My authority," God firmly commanded in June of 1981. It was my first seminar in London, and the night before, a scary awe had come over me as I looked over Westminster Hall, where the seminar was to be held for those 2,500 women. A tremendous reluctance swept over me at the thought of my having the audacity to tell these lovely ladies they needed to change.

The next morning, I asked God for His Word for me. While I was reading in Titus 2, He firmly assured me with His prerecorded answer: "These . . . are the things you should teach. Encourage and rebuke with all authority. Do not let anyone despise you" (verse 15).

From the time I started teaching, there was no sense of anything but God doing His great work in our midst; I had indescribable freedom to speak and exhort and reprove all that day because God had assured me of His authority with His prerecorded answer!

"I've just been waiting to share that secret with you," God eagerly answers my searching mind. And then my heart burns within me, as with the two on the Emmaus Road that first Easter (Luke 24:32), while He opens His treasure of wisdom and knowledge and pulls back the curtain on deep and exciting mysteries from His Word — mysteries that have been there since the foundation of the world but are just now mine — because I asked.

"I thought you'd never ask." Of all the ways God answers, this probably is the one He most often repeats. God almost sighs in relief as we finally get around to including Him in our search for advice and instruction. "But why did you wait so long," He sighs wearily, "when I had the answers ready for you all along?"

Yes, God's voices in answering me are as varied as my needs, frequently surprising me, but always giving me just what I need or deserve. God is not remote, speaking from somewhere up in the sky, but is always present with me while I turn to His Word for His answers.

> *Lord, I want to seek Your answers in all things.*
> *Please give me the wisdom to recognize the answers*
> *You've given in Your Word.*

MINDS BLINDED BY SATAN

And even if our Gospel is veiled, it is veiled to those who are perishing, in whose case the god of this world has blinded the minds of the unbelieving, that they might not see the light of the Gospel of the glory of Christ, who is the image of God.

2 Corinthians 4:3-4

A tactic of Satan about which we should pray is his *blinding the minds of those who are perishing* (2 Corinthians 4:3-4).

"The perishing" are those who are still in Satan's captivity because they have not been transferred out of Satan's kingdom into Jesus' kingdom at salvation. They are those who will spend eternity in hell with Satan instead of in heaven with Jesus.

And the "god of this world" is Satan. He is the one who has blinded the minds of unbelievers. Again, our sharing the Gospel will be in vain if their minds are blinded to it. So it is absolutely necessary to involve God *before* we try to win them to Jesus. We need to pray for God to remove the blinders Satan is keeping so securely in place on the lost.

God *does* open their minds. When Paul went to the riverside in Philippi looking for a place of prayer on the Sabbath, he found a group of women. As he taught them, the Lord opened Lydia's heart to respond to the things spoken by Paul (Acts 16:14). She became the first convert Paul won in Europe. But it was *the Lord* who opened Lydia's heart.

> ➤ *Dear Father, Open the minds and hearts of those who have been blinded by Satan. Lord, I know that anything I do will be in vain if You are not preparing them for Your Word.*

Walking Away from Sin

"Produce fruit in keeping with repentance."
Matthew 3:8

*T*urning away from sin is a step of true repentance. There is no real repentance without this step. For years, I have asked God daily to search my heart and show me my sins. And I find it relatively easy to admit that these un-Christlike attitudes and actions are sin and to ask for forgiveness. And I truly do regret having said, done, or thought certain things, but I do not actually repent until I turn away from them. Proverbs 28:13 says, "He who conceals his sins does not prosper, but whoever confesses and *renounces* them finds mercy" (emphasis mine).

The husband who sleeps with another woman every night and then asks to be forgiven the next day does not understand God's requirements. The only words God has for him are "Repent—and prove your repentance by a change of actions!"

True repentance is "[producing] *fruit in keeping with repentance*" (Matthew 3:8). It is not only turning from something, but also it is turning to something.

The word *repent* in Greek literally means to

change one's mind and to turn *from* sin and *to* God. As Jesus told the woman taken in adultery to "go, and sin no more" (John 8:11, NASB), it means a drastic turnabout in thinking and lifestyle.

This expected, drastic change in action applies to both the Christian and the non-Christian when they repent — the Christian reestablishing a God-pleasing lifestyle and the non-Christian embarking on one. Second Corinthians 7:8-10 shows us the Christian turning back to God, and Acts 26:20 shows the unbeliever turning to God.

There is a striking contrast in behavior when there is true repentance. A lifestyle just the opposite of the old one of sin emerges. The contrast is clearly described in Romans 6:12-13, "Therefore do not let sin reign in your mortal body so that you obey its evil desires. Do not offer the parts of your body to sin, as instruments of unrighteousness, but rather offer yourselves to God, as those who have been brought from death to life; and offer the parts of your body as instruments of righteousness." Repentance demands action. Don't just repent and repent. Get up from your knees and do something about it!

> *Lord, Help me to walk away from the sin*
> *I've repented of and go on to things which*
> *glorify Your Name.*

KEEP ALERT

Devote yourselves to prayer, being watchful and thankful.
Colossians 4:2

Occasionally, while in prayer, I slip from thankfulness into grumbling. It was at one of those times, while on vacation, that I recognized this attitude in me while reading Colossians 4:2, "Devote yourselves to prayer, keeping watchful and thankful."

Deeply rebuked, I cried out, "O God, forgive me. Bring me back to a right relationship with You. Make my testimony positive before others. I have taken my eyes off You. Replace my uptightness with your peace and joy—and thankfulness!" And it worked—as it always does!

Why do we have to keep alert in prayer? Because the Bible clearly tells us that Christians are in a spiritual battle and that we have an enemy, Satan.

In Ephesians 6, God describes the armor that will enable us to stand firm against the devil. But most of the time, we stop short of God's warning at the close, to be on the alert—in prayer. Verse 18 cautions: "Pray in the spirit on all occasions with all kinds of prayers and requests. With this in mind, be alert and always keep on praying for all the saints."

Obviously, Satan wants us to grumble, to be negative and powerless, thus destroying our own well-being and witness. However, being alert isn't one of the things we usually associate with prayer. But God does. He expects us to be fighting the only battle known where the soldiers go forth on their knees.

➤ *Lord, Keep me alert and give me an attitude of thankfulness when I'm at prayer. Help me to stand firm against satanic attack.*

THE EXAMPLE OF CHRIST

"Father, if You are willing, take this cup from Me;
yet not My will, but Yours be done."
Luke 22:42

The supreme example of praying in the will of God is that of Christ praying in the Garden of Gethsemane on the night before He was to die on the cross for our sins. Our Lord, in His humanity, did not want to suffer. He prayed, "Father, if You are willing, take this cup from Me; yet not My will, but Yours be done" (Luke 22:42). Then, after much agony of spirit, He said, "Father, I am willing for Your will."

Have you come to the place in your life where you can say, "Lord, not my will, but Thine be done. No matter how much it hurts, how difficult the task, how high the mountain You've given me to climb, it doesn't make any difference, dear Lord, I am willing"?

When we visited the Holy Land a few years ago, I sat alone under one of those old, gnarled olive trees in the Garden of Gethsemane and read in Luke's Gospel the account of all my Jesus went through the night before He died, before He took upon Himself the sin of the world, including mine;

when He sweat as it were great drops of blood there in the garden. With my heart absolutely breaking, I wrote in the margin of my Bible, "Lord, please, only Your will in my life, only Your will!" We don't have to sit under an ancient olive tree in His land to come to that place, but right where we are today we can say to Christ, "Lord, not my will, only Yours be done."

➤ *Lord, I want to do Your will. No matter what You ask of me, I want to obey Your leading in all things.*

"What Do You Mean, Repent?"

Humble yourselves before the Lord, and He will lift You up.
James 4:10

What is repentance? It involves three things: being truly sorrowful for the sin, actively turning away from that sin, and bringing forth fruit in keeping with repentance.

Being really sorry for the sin is to be absolutely devastated by the thought of it. It was when the men of Israel heard Peter raise his voice and recount their sins that they were "pierced to the heart" and cried out, asking the apostle what to do. Peter's reply was, "Repent!"

Repentance was my own father literally hitting his head against the wall because of what he had done to my mother. After years of being untrue to her when he traveled as a state highway contractor, he finally confessed his sin to her. Why did he confess? Because he saw his sin in contrast to my dear mother's holy life before God. When he came home from his week on the road, he told her he could almost see an angel hovering over her. It was her godlike holiness in contrast to his lustful wickedness that led him to confess—and change his lifestyle.

After acknowledging our sin comes the step of repentance—being horrified and devastated by the sinning and begging God for a clean heart.

The first prerequisite for prayer power in our lives that we study in my prayer seminars is "no known unconfessed sin in the life of the pray-er." Before we begin our first audible prayer time in small groups, I read a list of commonly practiced sins from the Bible—such as pride, lying, lust, wasting time, bitterness, money as our god, corrupt communication, and being a fake. As the Holy Spirit convicts us through God's Word, there almost always is deep repentance, with all confessing and many weeping.

Our sin may make us uncomfortable or even embarrassed, but Paul tells us that this process is good for us. After sending a letter to the Christians in Corinth condemning their sins, Paul wrote a second time, rejoicing in that godly sorrow that had produced repentance: "Even if I caused you sorrow by my letter, I do not regret it. Though I did regret—I see that my letter hurt you, but only for a little while—yet now I am happy, not because you were made sorry, but because your sorrow led you to repentance. For you became sorrowful as God intended and so were not harmed in any way by us" (2 Corinthians 7:8-9).

➢ *O Lord, I've seen the ugliness of my sin and I repent. I am overwhelmed with Your loving forgiveness. Thank You for providing a perfect sacrifice for my sin.*

OFFENSIVE PRAYING

The god of this age has blinded the minds of unbelievers,
so that they cannot see the light of the Gospel
of the glory of Christ.
2 Corinthians 4:4

How can we get God to open the hearts of those we are trying to win to Jesus? By praying. Though God is sovereign and moves as He pleases, prayer definitely activates God's working in unbelievers.

Second Corinthians 4:4 was the Scripture a close pastor friend used to break the hold Satan had on a medical doctor as he was struggling in the pastor's office. The doctor's search had taken him through a deep study of secular philosophies, and he had been trained in the doctrine of the church into which he was born. Finding inconsistencies and discrepancies in what they taught, he sought out my pastor friend.

"I can't believe. I want to, but I can't!" the doctor cried.

The pastor asked him if they could pause to pray. "In the middle of the prayer," the pastor told me, "I just said: 'In the Name of the Lord Jesus Christ, I bind Satan from blinding you to the light of the

Gospel of the glory of Christ.' "

As soon as the pastor finished praying, the doctor calmly said, "I want to receive Christ." And he did!

This is offensive spiritual warfare praying—asking God to remove Satan's veil that is blinding the minds of those we are trying to win to Jesus.

➢ *Lord, Remove the veil from _____'s mind so that _____ may come to know You. Prepare _____'s heart so that he/she can experience Your salvation.*

DRAW NEAR

Give ear to my words, O LORD, consider my sighing.
Listen to my cry for help, my King and my God,
for to You I pray. In the morning, O LORD,
You hear my voice; in the morning I lay my
requests before You and wait in expectation.
Psalm 5:1-3

Moses drew near to God when he "rose up early in the morning, and went up unto Mount Sinai" (Exodus 34:4, 29-35, NASB). Do you remember what happened when he came down? The Children of Israel were afraid to come near him because the skin of his face shone! He had to put a veil over his face, it was so radiant. Wouldn't it be great if we could draw so close to God that we would become radiant? So close that others could tell by our very countenance that we had been with God? That we had learned the secret of His presence? That before bombarding Him with our requests, we had taken time to enter into His fellowship?

For you to do:

1. Before starting to pray, in absolute silence practice drawing near to God. This may involve confessing some sin which God brings to your mind.

If so, confess it, so that there is nothing between you and God in heaven.

2. Now draw near to Him. Wait in silence until you feel God is there.

3. Now pray, thanking God for who He is— whatever you want to say in adoration and praise for who He is—this God to whom you have just drawn near.

4. Now pray at least one request for some other person's need.

➤ *O Lord, Help me to draw near to You*
as I come into Your presence in prayer.

PRAYER TRANSCENDS MILES

The LORD is near to all who call on Him,
to all who call on Him in truth.
Psalm 145:18

D o you have loved ones who live a great distance from you? Perhaps a son or a daughter who is away at school? In prayer we can sense a oneness that transcends the miles that separate us. God is not limited to space, as we are. He is able to reach down and give the unifying sense of His presence not only to people sitting beside us in the room but to individuals who are separated by continents. We proved this by an experiment in 1965.

After I had been praying with my two prayer partners every Thursday afternoon for almost a year, my husband and I went overseas to visit some mission fields. Before leaving we noted when we were scheduled to land in Addis Ababa, Ethiopia, where one of my prayer partner's daughter and son-in-law were stationed. Our arrival would be just prior to the corresponding time that my prayer partners would be meeting for prayer in Rockford, though there would be an eight-hour difference on the clock. We calculated that if all the planes were on schedule and if everything went according to plan, we would be in Addis Ababa to pray with her daughter and her husband at exactly the same time my prayer partners were praying in Rockford.

We arrived in Addis Ababa exhausted, but on schedule. After we were settled, the three of us went to pray in the living room. We had prayed for a short while when suddenly each of us had an overwhelming sense that no miles separated us and my two prayer partners back in Rockford. It was just as if they were right there praying with us. God had transcended all the miles across half the continent of the United States, the entire Atlantic Ocean, and most of the continent of Africa, and given to us a sense of oneness in His Spirit through prayer.

After we returned home, I was anxious to learn what happened in Rockford that Thursday afternoon. Had they felt that oneness that transcends the miles? My friend said to me then, and she has repeated it over and over since, "Ev, I have never in all my years as a Christian been so aware of God and His power, so aware of His reality, as I was when I sensed that tremendous unity we had in Him, even though we were separated by thousands of miles." This too is the horizontal dimension of prayer, linking the pray-ers through our omnipresent God.

> *Lord, Thank You that You transcend*
the miles that separate us and our loved ones.
Thank you that in prayer we can be together
with each other — and You.

Follow the Light

I am the light of the world. Whoever follows Me
will never walk in darkness, but will have the light of life.
John 8:12

When the blinding is removed from the mind of lost sinners, they can "see the light." Second Corinthians 4:4 says Satan blinds "so that the unbelieving cannot see the light of the Gospel of the glory of Christ." Satan is desperately trying to keep his captives from seeing the light of Jesus, *so one of his main tactics is to blind them to the light of Jesus.*

Again it is the battle between the *kingdom of darkness and the kingdom of light.* But Jesus came as the light of the world. The Prophet Isaiah prophesied, "The people who sit in darkness will see a great light" (Isaiah 9:2, NASB). Then the prophecy was fulfilled in Jesus. "The people living in darkness have seen a *great light"* (Matthew 4:16, emphasis added). Jesus!

> I am the light of the world. Whoever follows Me
> will never walk in darkness, but will have the light
> of life (John 8:12).

People are transferred out of the kingdom of darkness into the kingdom of light when they accept Jesus. The Christians in Ephesus were told, "you were formerly darkness, but now you are *light* in the Lord" (Ephesians 5:8, NASB, emphasis added).

In Paul's call on the Damascus road, Jesus said the purpose was "to open their eyes and *turn them from darkness to light,* and from the power of Satan to God" (Acts 26:18, emphasis added). However, those living in the kingdom of darkness do not see the Light because they are blinded by Satan. So what can we do about their not seeing the Light, Jesus? We can pray!

Praying for blinded eyes is offensively demanding that Satan remove the blinders. We must claim the blood and name of Jesus against Satan — and then ask God to bring the light of Jesus into them.

> ➤ *Lord, You are the Light of the world and the Light*
> *of my life! I pray for You to remove the blinders*
> *so that unbelievers still living in darkness*
> *would see Your glorious light and come to You.*
> *I pray that my life would also be a light*
> *which would guide the lost to You.*

WHY REPENT?

*Submit yourselves, then, to God. Resist the devil
and he will flee from you. Come near to God and
He will come near to you. Wash your hands, you sinners,
and purify your hearts, you double-minded.*

James 4:7-8

hy repent? Because I've seen myself as God
sees me.

Seeing ourselves as God sees us reveals our need
to repent. This came forcefully to me when we first
arrived at the cottage after Chris had surgery in
1982. Completely exhausted and frazzled, I had
dashed from my last speaking engagement at a convention to drive our car, with our boat in tow, to
our vacation spot. I struggled hour after hour,
pushing harder and harder to catch the car ferry we
were to take across Lake Michigan.

My husband, propped up on foam pillows next to
me in the car, kept giving me every little direction
for slowing down, turning, speeding up, and park-
ing. I found myself getting more and more edgy,
responding with short and sometimes rather unkind
answers. Our son and my husband's sister were
along, and I suddenly became aware of how I must
look in their eyes — and was not at all pleased.

However, the very next day as I took my Bible down to the beach for my early morning devotions, I saw something much more important than how they saw me. I was reading in the first chapter of 2 Peter, carefully observing the wonderful list of Christian attributes. While reading "make every effort to add to your faith goodness . . . godliness . . . brotherly kindness . . . love" (1:5-7), suddenly, the word *kindness* almost jumped out at me.

Then these words in the next two verses horrified me: "If you possess these qualities in increasing measure, they will keep you from being ineffective and unproductive in knowledge of our Lord Jesus Christ. But if anyone does not have them, he is nearsighted and blind, and has forgotten that he has been cleansed from his past sins" (2 Peter 1:8-10).

Suddenly, I saw myself as God saw me. Oh, how much more important this was than how other people saw me — even those dear to me! Weeping, I repented there alone on the deserted beach.

> *Lord, I am such a sinner!*
> *I repent of the evil within my heart.*

WHICH POSTURE?

*The eyes of the LORD are on the righteous
and His ears attentive to their cry.*
Psalm 34:15

J ust as prayer requires no particular place, neither does it require a certain prayer posture. In one of our seminars a man announced to me after the first session that he would not be back. "You're not praying scripturally," he said. When I asked him to please explain, he replied, "You're not 'holding up holy hands.' " He could see only this one position to be used at all times, even though I pointed out to him that there are many postures of prayer mentioned in the Word of God.

When Jesus was praying in the Garden of Gethsemane, He gave us the example of *kneeling* in prayer. "He withdrew from them about a stone's throw beyond them, knelt down and prayed" (Luke 22:41). At the tomb of Lazarus, while standing, "Jesus looked up, and said, 'Father, I thank You that You have heard Me' " (John 11:41). Paul wrote, "I want men everywhere *to lift up holy hands in prayer,* without anger and disputing" (1 Timothy 2:8).

My husband can recall circumstances in which

men experienced such grief and anguish that they lay prostrate on the floor of his study. One was a dad who had just learned that his teenage daughter was pregnant out of wedlock. He cast himself to the floor, weeping, and my husband had to take him in his arms and gently lift him up.

King Solomon, in the Old Testament, *prostrated himself before the Lord* when he prayed in the temple. His father, David, communed with God upon his bed (Psalm 4:4). Whatever our posture, wherever the place, the ears of our God are open to our cry (see Psalm 34:15).

➤ *Dear Father, Thank You for listening to my prayers, no matter where I am or what bodily posture I use.*

HINDRANCES TO
ACCEPTING GOD'S ANSWERS

*But if from there you seek the LORD your God,
you will find Him if you look for Him
with all your heart and with all your soul.*
Deuteronomy 4:29

God has prerecorded the answers to most of the questions we ask Him in prayer. Unfortunately, we have built up within ourselves hindrances to receiving His prerecorded answers.

Disbelief in the authenticity of the Bible frequently keeps people from believing God's prerecorded answers. Disbelief in the authority of God's Word also can be a stumbling block to accepting His prerecorded answers.

Theological hang-ups can also hinder our acceptance of God's answers to our prayers. Most of us are hemmed in by a theological system either from the denomination into which we were born, the church we chose as an adult, or from gullibly accepting it.

Rebellion. Even though we agree theologically with God's answer and know we should accept it, many times we rebel against His will for us and are too stubborn to accept His prerecorded answer.

Not applying it personally is also a hindrance to the effectiveness in our lives of God's prerecorded answers. It is far easier to apply that reproof, correction, or instruction to the ones we are teaching, our congregation, or even our mates, children, or acquaintances. But it is only as we are willing to accept His answer for us personally that it can accomplish that which God intended it to do when He recorded it. "Blessed are those who hear the word of God and observe it" (Luke 11:28, NASB).

> *Dear Father, Fill me with the faith I need to accept Your answers. Please give me the strength to recognize any hindrances and courage to apply Your answers in my life daily.*

INTERACT WITH THE AUTHOR

The Word of God is living and active.
Hebrews 4:12

S ince God is personally present when we receive His answers from the Bible, it is logical that He expects us to interact with Him about what He has said. And since this is the only book in which the author is always present while it is being read, it also is true that this is the only book where a personal interaction with the Author, God, is necessary.

The Bible differs from all other books ever written in that it is alive. Hebrews 4:12 says "The Word of God is living and active. Sharper than any double-edged sword . . . it judges the thoughts and attitudes of the heart." This is only possible because God Himself, its Author, is active in its convicting, enlightening, and instructing process. Thus, the Bible can be applied practically only through spiritual involvement with God Himself. And this interaction is prayer.

There are three steps necessary in using God's Word effectively: (1) accept it, (2) respond to its Author, and (3) live it. We frequently want to bypass number two and resolutely set our jaws and grit our teeth declaring, "I will not," or stoically set out to obey its commands. But it is only when we involve the Author of these rules and instructions that we receive the wisdom, grace, strength, power and, most important, the desire to apply them.

We must respond personally to God about what He has said to us — asking forgiveness for that specific sin, staying quietly in His presence while He cleanses us, seeing ourselves in contrast to His holiness, imploring Him to make us more like the Jesus He just showed us.

There is no other author who discerns and judges the thoughts and the intents of our hearts and scrutinizes the spiritual, emotional, and intellectual aspects of our lives. Nor do we stand before any other author stripped and bare and fully exposed, with nothing concealed (Hebrews 4:13). Thus, no other book consistently and without fail can have prerecorded answers for the immediate and specific needs of the reader, for no other author is actively involved in the inmost and hidden self of the reader.

To be confronted by God's answers in the Bible is to be confronted by God Himself.

➤ *Father, Forgive me for neglecting to read*
the Bible for Your answers to my prayers. Teach me
to submerge myself in Your instructions and commands
for me and then to interact with You about them.
Lord, I now promise You I will seek, accept, and obey
Your answers for me.

A Servant of God

"Blessed is she who has believed that what the Lord has said to her will be accomplished!"

1 Thessalonians 5:17, NASB

Mary had a tremendous privilege because she was willing for God's will in her life. Do you recall her response at the time of the Annunciation? When the angel came to her and said that God had chosen her to be the mother of the Savior, Mary immediately responded, "I am the Lord's servant. . . . May it be to me as you have said."

Do you think it was easy for Mary to say yes to the will of God, being pregnant out of wedlock? When it meant vulnerability to misunderstanding, to ridicule? When it could mean possible rejection by her fiancé or even being stoned to death? It was not easy for Mary, but because she was willing for God's will, she was greatly blessed by Him. She was given the great privilege of bearing the Son who became our Redeemer.

Has God put before you an open door? Are you hesitating, perhaps rebelling, or holding back because of fear, when God is challenging, "Look, here's an open door, wouldn't you like to walk through it for Me? This is My will for you"?

Oh, answer Him, "Lord, here I am. There is no friction between my will and Yours. Whatever You have for me, I know that You will give me enough strength, enough grace. I know You will give me all that I need. Lord, I am ready to do your will."

> *O God, I want only Your will in my life.*
Open the doors You have for me, and give me the
courage and faith to go through them.

EXCEEDING ABUNDANTLY

. . . to Him that is able to do immeasurably more
than all that we ask or imagine. . . .
Ephesians 3:20

I have not expected most of the dramatic answers from God in this prayer ministry. When we started, I didn't even know if my church women would pray with me and, if they did, if God would do anything. But now, with God's overwhelming responses, I know! But I also have become painfully aware of all the good things God desires to pour out on Planet Earth, which I limit Him from doing because I do not pray enough.

Dr. Paul Yonggi Cho, pastor of a now 1 million-member church in Seoul, Korea, said to us while explaining the power for that kind of church growth, "Americans stay after church and eat. We stay after church and pray." I mentioned this at a recent pastors' conference. We then went to prayer, and one pastor blurted out, "O God, I don't pray enough. Forgive my lack of prayer—my personal prayer, prayer with my family, prayer for my church. O God, forgive me!" Surprisingly, almost no American seminaries teach for credit on the subject of prayer's power. But prayer is the key that unlocks God's omnipotent throne room.

In Ephesians 3:20, Paul gives us a tremendous look into God's mind. And I have found that life bathed in, saturated by, and directed through prayer has been exhilarating and exciting. I feel as if I'm continuously standing on tiptoe, straining to peer into God's mind, wondering how and what He is going to do this time. Yes, I have learned about His doing "immeasurably more than [any of us could] ask or imagine" when we prayed.

Capable, yes. And able too—when there is enough prayer! How much power is God releasing because of your prayers? Then again, how much power is God waiting for you to unlock with your key of prayer?

> *O God, I confess that there is not enough power from prayer in my life. Father, You are not able to do many of the things You desire to do here on Earth because of my lack of praying. I long to see Your exceeding, abundant answers over and above anything I could ask or think. Lord, I commit myself to spend more time in prayer daily. Help me to discipline myself to more actual praying.*

Calling with a Pure Heart

Flee the evil desires of youth,
and pursue righteousness, faith, love and peace,
along with those who call on the Lord out of a pure heart.
2 Timothy 2:22

One of the prayer requests presented at a faculty wives' prayer meeting I attended involved a serious financial problem. On the day before the prayer meeting, the promise of a large gift of money for the new campus had been withdrawn, and now we were going to pray about it.

As we were chatting before the start of the prayer meeting, a woman came in whom I had never met. I didn't know who she was, but I looked down my spiritual nose and thought, "My word, she's the strangest woman I've ever seen in my life." And the more she talked, the stranger I thought she was.

Then the Lord began to reprove me, "Evelyn, that's sin." Do you remember the prerequisite to answered prayer? "If I regard iniquity in my heart, the Lord will not hear me." I suddenly realized that I was about to spend my morning in prayer with sin in my heart! Another SOS Prayer flew to heaven, "Lord, please give me the attitude You want me to have toward that woman, whoever she is."

When we pray that prayer, we never ask amiss. God knows what attitude He wants to give us. When we look at Christ's life, we can see that sometimes His perfect attitude was love, and sometimes it was righteous indignation, patience, discipline, or compassion.

That day God gave me a surprise. Guess who prayed first at that prayer meeting? She did. And as she started to pray, I suddenly realized that this woman had a dimension to her prayer life that I knew nothing about. She said, "Thank You, Lord, that the money didn't come through yesterday." She went on, "Now, Lord, You have given us the privilege of being on our faces before You this morning with a desperate need. Lord, what a privilege this is. Thank You, Lord. And thank You that today the school's president has the privilege of being on his face before You with this need. Thank You that the whole staff has this tremendous need, and thank You that they have the privilege of being on their faces before You."

I felt two inches high. When I learned who this woman was, I discovered some other things. She had intercessory prayer life that was never less than two hours a day. She used a prayer list that was pages and pages long, containing the names of the people for whom she prayed daily. And I had looked at her and thought, "Wow, is she strange!"

> *Lord, I want to come before You*
> *with a clean mind and heart.*

AN OMNISCIENT FATHER

So then, those who suffer according to God's will should commit themselves to their faithful Creator and continue to do good.

1 Peter 4:19

I s your God an all-wise Father, who knows the end from the beginning, who knows all the causes and all the outcomes, and who never makes a mistake? We may pray for something that seems very good to us, but God knows the "what ifs" in our lives. He knows the calamities that might occur if He answered our prayers in the way we think best. He also knows about all our difficult situations and wants to turn them into something tremendously good.

This view of God as an omniscient Father comes into focus very clearly as the years pass. One of the advantages of growing older is that we can look back and see that God has not made a single mistake in our lives. Maybe we'll have to get to heaven before we understand some things, but it's exciting to recognize as the years come and go that God has worked everything for good if we have really loved Him. When we keep a record of what is happening to us, it isn't long before we realize that the difficult things are there for a reason, and God is making no mistakes.

When we're bringing our requests to Him, we're saying, "Lord, here's the need"—the circumstance, the person, whatever it may be; then we ask Him to answer according to His omniscient will—knowing it always will be for our best.

I'm not being a pawn on a chessboard if I say willingly, "Lord, I really don't know what the best for me would be. But, Lord, You know all the 'what ifs' and all the outcomes. So, Lord, when hard things and even suffering comes into my life, I know You will work everything out for my good."

➤ *Dear Father, Help me to trust Your guidance in my life. Thank You that You care enough to answer my prayers in the way You know will be best for me.*

ASKING WITH
WRONG MOTIVES?

*When you ask, you do not receive
because you ask with wrong motives. . . .*
James 5:3

How can we be sure that we are not praying with improper motives? James writes, "When you ask, you do not receive, because you ask with wrong motives, that you may spend what you get on your pleasures" (James 4:3). Let's never insult God by saying, "O Lord, that other woman's husband looks just a little bit good to me. Is it okay if I just sit at his feet—in my imagination? There won't be anything physical about our relationship, Lord." Let's not ever ask whether that can be God's will. We know what His will is, for He says, "Be ye holy for I am holy."

Perhaps we say, "Lord, look at that new car, that new house," or "Wow! Look at her wardrobe, Lord! It is all right if I'm just a little bit jealous?" Now, we don't really ask God such questions, but we often rationalize our feelings and attitudes in an attempt to justify them, don't we?

It may be that we're a little bit touchy. We whimper and complain, "Lord, she rubs me the wrong way. Look at what she did. I really don't like her very much. Could that be Your will, Lord?" No. God's Word says, "Love does not demand its own way. It is not irritable or touchy" (1 Corinthians 13:5, TLB). So one sure way of asking with the right motives is to know God's Word, the Bible. If God calls it sin, don't insult Him by asking about it.

There is nothing in God's Word that is contrary to God's will. If we find God's "no" in His Word, we should believe it, accept it, and act accordingly.

> ➤ Lord, Forgive me for even asking if You could
> allow those things in my life. You have said
> they are off-limits for me — and they are sin.

You Cannot Deceive God

Do not be deceived: God cannot be mocked.
A man reaps what he sows. The one who sows
to please his sinful nature, from that nature
will reap destruction; the one who sows to please
the Spirit, from the Spirit will reap eternal life.
Galatians 6:7-8

What would happen to our moral standards if, every time there was a temptation to any degree, we would cry out as Joseph did, "How then could I do such a wicked thing and sin against God?" (Genesis 39:9) Joseph saw himself as God saw him. Do we?

Somehow, we feel that if we can deceive those around us, no one will know of our sin. Also, we think we can fool those against whom we are sinning, although this usually is not true either. However, we never deceive God. David, before praying his famous "Search me, O God" at the close of Psalm 139, opens it with "O Lord, Thou hast searched me and known me. . . . Even before there is a word on my tongue, behold, O Lord, Thou dost know it all" (verses 1-4, NASB). The writer of Hebrews expresses the same thought, "Nothing in all creation is hidden from God's sight. Everything is uncovered and laid bare before the eyes of Him to whom we must give account" (Hebrews 4:13).

Denial of our sin sometimes is a protective shield we build around ourselves to keep from getting hurt. In the self-protection of the denial, we justify the self-preservation instead of seeing the denial as God sees it — as sin. But denial actually produces the sin of "deceit," found in so many lists of sins in the Bible. Denial, of course, is lying (itself a biblical sin). Then one lie demands another, and then another, to keep covering up the original lie — until there is a hopeless web of deceit which we have spun around ourselves.

When we stop denying and start admitting that what we are doing or have done is sin, then we are able to admit it to others — who most likely knew it anyway — and to God — who positively did know it anyway. Paul was addressing Christians when he wrote, "Do not be deceived: God cannot be mocked. A man reaps what he sows. The one who sows to please his sinful nature, from that nature will reap destruction; the one who sows to please the Spirit, from the Spirit will reap eternal life" (Galatians 6:7-8).

> *Lord, Forgive me for my deceptiveness. I may be able to fool people on earth, but You always know what's going on inside of me. Father, help me to see my deceptiveness as You see it — as sin.*

We Had Never Met

For this reason, since the day we heard about you,
we have not stopped praying for you and asking God
to fill you with knowledge of His will through all
spiritual wisdom and understanding.
Colossians 1:9

P rayer can create a bond—even among people who have never met. One of the ladies in our prayer chain went to another state to purchase a poodle from a woman named Joy. She had had major surgery involving the insertion of a plastic esophagus, and was having an extremely difficult pregnancy. It was no wonder that our prayer chain member came back and said, "Let's pray for Joy." We started, and week after week, month after month, we prayed for her.

One day, after Joy delivered her baby, she told her husband that it was only because those women down there in Rockford were praying that she had the strength and the courage to get through her pregnancy. And that was not all—this dear woman accepted Christ as her personal Savior, and became the best missionary we ever had! Everyone who came to buy a poodle heard that she had found Christ and was told about the women many miles away who had prayed and prayed for her physical and spiritual needs. To this day I haven't met Joy. It isn't likely that I will, for I don't think I'll ever buy a poodle. But God answered anyway!

On our prayer chain lists are many whom we have never met, but God knows who they are and where they are. He knows their needs. All we do is pray our requests—we don't pray answers—and with the mighty arm of His power, God reaches down to anyone anywhere on Planet Earth with His answers.

➤ *Lord, Thank You for the strength You have given us through prayer. Keep me diligent in my prayers for those I don't see every day—or may never see at all.*

GOD IS THE REWARDER

. . . without faith it is impossible to please God,
because anyone who comes to Him must believe
that He exists and that He rewards those
who earnestly seek Him.

Hebrews 11:6

M uch happens when we pray. And answers come as we pray in faith believing. We come first of all believing that God is, and then believing unequivocally that He rewards those who seek Him. "But without faith it is impossible to please God, because anyone who comes to Him must believe that He exists and that He rewards those who earnestly seek Him" (Hebrews 11:6).

As we pray believingly, we see a result in the horizontal dimension of prayer—it is great in its working. We are not dropping our prayers into a bottomless barrel. How do we know? One way is by the specific answers to specific requests. Early in our prayer ministry, we began to experience great answers to prayer. At my very first prayer seminar in White Bear Lake, a woman handed me a request for our intercessory prayer time. It was for her sister to receive Christ. She said, "We've tried everything we know. We've talked to her; we've taken her to meetings where she's spurned invitation after invitation to receive Him. Please pray." Though they did not even know her name, 250 women zeroed in on that unsaved sister.

The next week the woman who had requested prayer stopped me before the seminar. "Do you know what? I took my sister to a Christian Women's Club luncheon right after the seminar last week, and she accepted Christ within two hours of your praying!" Those 250 pray-ers gave great praise during prayer time that day.

What happens when we pray? Things do happen. We do not drop our intercessory prayers into a bottomless barrel. We send them up to a Heavenly Father, who in His time, in His way, according to His will, answers them down here on Planet Earth.

➢ *Lord, Thank You for Your answers to prayer! Your goodness is beyond my comprehension!*

If Only

Create in me a pure heart, O God,
and renew a steadfast spirit within me.
Psalm 51:10

When there has been a devastating sin in our lives, we say, "If only! What if I had not done it? What would I be, what could I have accomplished if only I had not sinned?" These are bitter words that plague the repentant sinner, causing seemingly never-ending shudders of the soul—"If only!"

David, even though forgiven by God, for the rest of his life paid the price for his sin against Bathsheba and her husband. God said the child she was bearing would die—and he did (2 Samuel 12:10-14). Also, David was not allowed to build the temple, and his family had to live by the sword from that time on. In his deep repentance, David often must have thought, *Oh, if only! If only I had not done it!* But, wonderfully, while we are crying "If only!" God is answering "Since." He answers our "if only" lament with, "Now then, since you have been forgiven, I am in charge of restoring your ministry."

David, after his deep repentance, found a very important word—then. Psalm 51 tells us that he bowed down acknowledging his sin, deeply repented of it, begged God to create in him a clean heart, and asked Him to restore the joy of His salvation. *"Then,"* David said, "I will teach transgressors Your ways, and sinners will turn back to You" (Psalm 51:13). Restored ministry!

And incredibly, God still used that repentant, restored sinner's lineage to produce the Messiah, Jesus! The New Testament opens with these words, "A record of the genealogy of Jesus Christ the son of David, the son of Abraham" (Matthew 1:1).

However, we must add that there is no way to know what glorious things God had planned for David had he not sinned. C.S. Lewis in his novel *Perelandra* said it like this, "Whatever you do, He will make good of it. But not the good He had prepared for you if you had obeyed Him. That is lost for ever." (C.S. Lewis, *Perelandra* [New York: Macmillan Co., 1958], 125.) We never will know what David's later life would have been without his horrible sin.

Many people have said to me, "God never can use me again because of that awful sin I committed." But God not only forgives when there is genuine repentance, He can restore, to the extent He chooses, status and position in His kingdom. We can be cleansed again for His holy ministry as He sees fit.

> *Dear Father, Thank You for forgiving my sins. But keep me constantly aware of the price I may pay for my sinning in missed future good.*

You Have Not Fulfilled My Requirements

. . . if My people, who are called by My name,
will humble themselves and pray and seek My face and
turn from their wicked ways, then I will hear
from heaven and will forgive their sin
and will heal their land.

2 Chronicles 7:14

Have you ever wondered why God answers no to some of your prayers? He may be saying, "You have not fulfilled My requirements. You do not qualify for My answer!" This is the greatest secret of unanswered prayer.

First John 3:22 gives us one of God the Father's basic rules for answering or not answering our prayers. It is the Father's "then":

And whatsoever we ask, we receive of Him, because we keep His commandments, and do those things that are pleasing in His sight (NASB).

The Father's approval or disapproval of our actions determines whether or not He will grant our prayer requests. Since both words *keep* and *do* in this verse of Scripture are in the continuous present tense in the Greek, power in prayer is conditioned not by an occasional burst of obedience but by lives that consistently please Him. *Then* He promises that we will receive that for which we ask.

One of the numerous "thens" in Scripture that determines answered prayer is in 2 Chronicles 7:14. God told Solomon that if His people would "humble themselves, pray, seek [His] face, and turn from their wicked ways; then [He would] hear from heaven, and [would] forgive their sin, and [would] heal their land." When they did, then He would.

David, after his deep sin with Bathsheba, knew and prayed God's *then* principle for the return of fruitfulness in his life. He was aware of the order God required. When he acknowledged his sin, deeply repented, begged God to create in him a clean heart, and asked God to restore the joy of His salvation—only *then* could he again teach transgressors of God's ways and sinners would be converted (Psalm 51).

We seem to be unaware of God's "thens" when we pray. But the Bible clearly tells us that God can answer our prayers only when we have been willing to be and to do what He requires. "When you keep my commandments and do the things which are pleasing in My sight," says the Lord, "Only then will you receive that for which you have asked" (see 1 John 3:22).

➤ *Lord, Open my eyes to the sin in my life*
so that I may confess and be pleasing in Your sight—
so that my prayers can be answered.

THE RESTORER IS GOD

*. . . if someone is caught in a sin,
you who are spiritual should restore him gently.*
Galatians 6:1

For nine months I lifted up and prayed for someone I needed to restore to fellowship. But when I was suddenly told the details of how the sinning had been against me, I felt a deep, tearing wound inside me. Then as I continued to struggle for another year in the restoring process, the burden seemed to become unbearable. And I bowed my head and sobbed, "O God, who restores the restorer?"

Astonishingly, God's answer immediately filled my mind. "It's the Twenty-third Psalm," He said. Assurance flooded my soul. There it was: *"He* restoreth my soul!" God!

Restoring the restorer was part of God's original intention when He instructed us to restore the fallen ones. Before telling us to "restore such a one," in Galatians 6:1, He already knew it would include His having to restore us—the restorers. Amazingly, "restore such a one" is in the continuous present Greek tense, suggesting a process of perhaps long duration, not just a once-for-all action.

Then, at the end of this portion of Scripture on restoring, God gives a promise. My heart leapt within me as I read, "Let us not become weary in doing good, for at the proper time we will reap a harvest if we do not give up" (Galatians 6:9).

It is admirable and tremendously helpful if the repentant sinner spends time and effort trying to make restitution to the one against whom he or she has sinned. The loving tenderness, the myriad of kind words and actions to make up for the hurting they caused are wonderful and do help so much. But the deep hole that we feel has been punched right in the middle of us only can be restored to wholeness by God. It is only God who can fill the devastating void left by severed relationships with children, relatives, and friends and by broken marriage vows. Only God can restore the *soul*.

➤ *Lord, Give me the grace and strength to restore those who have wronged me. Thank You, Lord, that You are the One who restores me in this difficult task.*

Now Obey Me

Dear friends, if our hearts do not condemn us,
we have confidence before God and receive from Him
anything we ask, because we obey His commands
and do what pleases Him.
1 John 3:21

What happens when God answers prayer? What God always expects to happen — our obedience.

After God has answered our prayer — whether exciting, mind-boggling — or difficult, the next step is obedience. When God answers our prayer with a command, instruction, or an open door, He fully expects us to obey. We must put into practice what God has told us in His answer. And our obedience to His answer to our prayer opens the curtain on the next act of our lives. "So is My word that goes out from My mouth: It will not return to Me empty, but will accomplish what I desire and achieve the purpose for which I sent it" (Isaiah 55:11).

This is the God of the universe speaking, the One whom all the stars, planets, weather, and seasons obey. The One who spoke, and the universe came into being. The One who spoke, and the sea was calm. Who spoke, and the dead came alive.

The One who expects obedience to His words.

However, God does not coerce us into obeying His answers to our prayers. He has given each of us a free will, with the privilege of responding as we choose. And, astoundingly, we humans frequently ignore, rebel, make excuses, refuse to obey, or even laugh at a certain answer from Him. This is amazing in light of the fact that it is the omniscient God of the universe who has answered us.

Our son, Kurt, said it to me this way: "Remember, when dealing with the Great Potter, the quality of the pot is solely determined by the malleability of the clay." It is our ability and willingness as clay to be shaped by God, the Potter, that ultimately fashions what we are — and what God can do through us.

> ➢ *Lord, Help me to be as clay — ready and willing to be conformed to Your will. Teach me to obey Your answers to my prayers, because I know You are fashioning me into that pot which will glorify and be used by You.*

You Haven't Finished the Task Yet

Wake up! Strengthen what remains and is about to die,
for I have not found your deeds complete
in the sight of my God.
Revelation 3:2

Obedience is not just an occasional burst of obeying God. The Apostle John wrote in 1 John 3:22 that we have power in prayer "because we obey His commands and do what pleases Him." And the words *keep* and *do* are in continuous tenses, meaning that we keep on keeping His commandments and doing the things that please Him.

Obedience is ongoing, not just one quick act. It involves stick-to-it-iveness, tenaciously persevering as long as God does not withdraw the call or command.

The first night of our International Prayer Assembly in Seoul, Korea, God reminded me powerfully to "complete the work you have received in the Lord" (Colossians 4:17).

Then at the end of that summer, I was feeling emotionally and physically exhausted, and I was reluctant to keep going full time with seminars and writing, plus such a full family life. I even had discussed with my husband how I might pull back.

For that September's United Prayer Ministries annual retreat, God had directed me to use Revelation 2 and 3. As I was preparing from these chapters, He abruptly spoke to me out of 3:2, "Wake up, and strengthen the things that remain, which were about to die; for I have not found your deeds complete in the sight of my God" (NASB).

You may think you are done, but God doesn't see your task completed. He is not finished with you yet!

> ➤ *Lord, I want to serve You as long as You choose.*
> *Forgive me for ever thinking my work for You is done*
> *just because I'm tired or overworked.*

NOT DOING?

"For I know the plans that I have for you,"
declares the Lord, "plans to prosper you and
not harm you, plans to give you a hope and future."
Jeremiah 29:11

One of the most difficult aspects of obedience is being willing *not* to do something. Obedience isn't only going and doing, it also is not going and not doing! This is especially hard when we feel that the job or activity is so right and so necessary.

There is an important step to take in most major tasks to which I feel God is calling me. After the excitement and emotional thrill have died down, I pray a different kind of prayer: "Lord, I give this back to You — not to do it — if that is Your will." These are not just mouthed words but a total submission of my whole being to what He wants.

This prayer helps avoid many wrong turns on the road of life. It eliminates much overextending of ourselves in doing things which humanly seem so right, but can be disastrous to His plans for us. Jeremiah said it so well: " 'For I know the plans that I have for you,' declares the Lord, 'plans to prosper you and not harm you, plans to give you a hope and future' " (29:11).

Paul must have been surprised and even confused when the Spirit did not permit him to speak the Word to those in Asia when he was so convinced that they needed to hear of Jesus. But God's plan was so right, and Paul's obedience opened Europe to the Gospel.

Also, when a position or job would bring prestige, honor, and favorable exposure to the world, it is especially hard to release it back to God. But when we are willing to decrease so that He and His kingdom may increase—this is real obedience.

Surprisingly for me, it frequently is *only* after I have prayed that prayer of release that God flings the door open wide to what He originally called me to do. To God, my complete obedience seems to include being willing not to do it; and then He says, "Now go!"

➤ *Lord, I know the plans You have for me are best. Forgive me for all the times I have stubbornly gone my own way. Teach me to give back each open door—not to do it if it is not Your will.*

Attitude of Gratitude

Give thanks in all circumstances,
for this is God's will for you in Christ Jesus.
1 Thessalonians 5:18

T hanksgiving is a lifestyle. Long before He answers, God requires an attitude of thanksgiving. "Devote yourselves to prayer, keeping alert in it with an attitude of thanksgiving" (Colossians 4:2, NASB, emphasis mine).

Our ultimate goal is to be engulfed by, saturated with, and completely controlled by an attitude of gratitude. Not some emotional high, or an escape from reality, but the actual living in a state of thankfulness—before, during, and after we receive answers to our prayers.

Paul explains in 1 Thessalonians 5:18 that this is not an option, but it is God's will for us, "Give thanks in all circumstances, for this is God's will for you in Christ Jesus" (NASB). While we are in every situation and while we are praying about it, we are to be thankful. Thanks should not have to be legislated through God's Word, but it should be the spontaneous response of our whole being toward Him.

I shivered in my hotel room in Australia one

winter Sunday evening. Chills from a flulike sore throat, plus sitting all that day in buildings with so much less heat than I was used to in America, left me miserable. Alone in that room, I kept getting sicker and sicker. I took a bite of an apple, but my throat hurt too much to swallow it. And I was scheduled to speak all day, starting early the next morning!

Knowing that no doctor could cure me fast enough for the next day's seminar, I just knelt down by my bed to pray. But I didn't panic, I didn't ask God to get a replacement speaker ready, I didn't even ask to be healed. No, rather I just stayed there, kneeling in prayer with my whole being wrapped in His presence—with feelings of thanks spontaneously flowing to God—thanks for the privilege of once again being absolutely dependent upon Him.

I wasn't asking for or expecting what resulted from that prayer, but rising from my knees, I was surprised to find my throat completely healed. Filled with an attitude of gratitude while praying— before He answered!

➤ *Father, I want to have an attitude of gratitude*
in all things. Give me the maturity to trust You enough
to be thankful while I am praying, not just after
You give me Your answer.

ACCEPT RESPONSIBILITY

If anyone sins and is unfaithful to the LORD
by deceiving his neighbor about something
entrusted to him or left in his care or stolen,
or if he cheats him, or . . . commits any such sin
that people may do — when he thus sins and becomes
guilty . . . . He must make restitution in full. . . .
Leviticus 6:2-5

When I teach the biblical responsibility of the one sinned against to forgive *(What Happens When Women Pray)* and what the serious consequences are to us if we don't forgive *(Gaining through Losing)*, people say to me, "But what about them?" Well, this reading is about "them" — the responsibility of the sinner who has caused the hurt.

Basically, it is the selfishness of the one sinning that causes the hurt the victim must endure. The current popular philosophy even among some Christians is to think only of being fulfilled themselves, doing what feels good, with little or no concern for those they may be hurting. It is the philosophy of humanism, or so-called Christian humanism, by which these Christians are living diametrically opposed to God's biblical rules.

Sinners must see themselves as the wrongdoers.

They must accept the fact that they are guilty of having hurt another person or perhaps many others. The one who has caused the emotional, mental, and perhaps physical suffering must accept responsibility for the one he or she has devastated — realizing that this person needs to be healed and that restitution is imperative.

Have you sinned by stealing someone else's reputation by passing on false or only partially true rumors about them? Have you undermined a minister God has called because of your vicious criticism of him? Have you destroyed somebody else's self-worth because this was the only way you could feed and satisfy your own pride and ego? Have you gotten ahead and succeeded by trampling a coworker? Is your sin with someone of the opposite sex, in thought or deed, devastating your mate? Is your child's emotional well-being shattered because you are selfishly living in sin? Are you causing anguish and undeserved guilt in your parents because of your lifestyle? Is stepping on somebody else the only way you can get what you want and what fulfills you? Then restitution to that person is in order.

> *Lord, Forgive me for the sins I have committed. Show me who is suffering because of my sinning. Give me the strength and courage to make restitution to those I have hurt.*

Believe in the Name of God

I write these things to you who believe
in the name of the Son of God
so that you may know that you have eternal life.
1 John 5:13

A member of our church in Rockford was one of our neighborhood Bible study teachers. She astounded us one Sunday by announcing that she had discovered during her own Bible study that she really did not know Jesus. "After twenty-nine years of prenatal care," she said, "I was born."

In my prayer seminars after reading my list of twenty-three scriptural sins and questions, which include "Are you a fake, just pretending to be a real Christian?" God powerfully breaks down cultural inhibitions, reservations, and their "never do it that way" excuses as they pray to accept Jesus. Sometimes, everyone just seems to explode, all praying aloud in their groups at once; and at other times, they continue one by one all over the room, as they did once for twelve minutes in Bristol, England. In a recent seminar of 2,700 people, it sounded as if two thirds prayed aloud simultaneously, making sure they had a personal relationship with Jesus.

It is likely that some of those praying may already be real Christians but are just not sure about their personal relationship with Jesus. The Bible tells us we can be sure. With a prayer of repentance and by accepting Jesus, we can join the ranks of those assured of their reconciliation with God from that state of sin into which we were all born, "I write these things to you who believe in the name of the Son of God so that you may know that you have eternal life (1 John 5:13).

When you ask Jesus, on the final Judgment Day, "Lord, when did I not visit You in prison, feed You, and so on?"—how will you handle it if Jesus answers, "Depart from Me, You who are cursed"? (Matthew 25:41) What a horrifying answer this will be for those who have only been cultural Christians, who belonged to fine churches or thought they were God's grandchildren because they had believing parents.

➤ *Lord, Am I a cultural Christian or a true believer? Jesus, I want to be sure that I have a personal relationship with You. If by any chance You are not living in me, come in as my Savior and my Lord.*

His Holy Presence

But now He has reconciled you by Christ's physical body through death to present you holy in His sight, without blemish and free from accusation.
Colossians 1:22

S o few Christians are even aware that they are not reconciled to God. It comes as a complete shock that while they are living in sin, although He still loves them, God certainly doesn't like them.

When I feel far from God and pray, "Father, I long for a deeper, closer walk with You," God answers me with "My child, you have broken our fellowship with your sin. You must be reconciled to Me first."

When my efforts as a reconciler of the world to God are ineffective and in frustration I ask God why, He frequently insists, "You must be reconciled to Me first!"

When I pray, "Lord, give me power in prayer," He sometimes answers literally, "Since you are regarding iniquity in your heart, I cannot hear you" (see Psalm 66:18). "Repent and let Me reconcile you once again to Myself—and reestablish our powerful relationship."

The only reason God convicts Christians of sin and demands repentance is so that we can be reconciled to Him and once again experience fellowship with Him. It is so that we can step into that room marked *His holy presence.* "Who may ascend into the hill of the Lord? Who may stand in His holy place? He who has clean hands and a pure heart" (Psalm 24:3-4).

Yes, when we have sinned, our part is to repent — and God's part is to reconcile us to Himself.

When God answers, "I forgive you and have reconciled you back to Myself," we step into the rare privilege of being, uninhibited and unrestrained, in the very presence of the Holy God of the universe. All hindrances to His presence are swept away, and we walk hand in hand with Him — just as if we never had sinned! "But now He has reconciled you by Christ's physical body through death to present you holy in His sight, without blemish and free from accusation" (Colossians 1:22).

O God, I confess that I have violated Your
holiness and, thus, our relationship is broken.
Please, God, cleanse me from all known and unknown sin.
And thank You, Father, for being holy enough
to be angry at my sin — but loving enough to forgive
me and to reconcile me to Yourself.

BE RECONCILED TO OTHERS

*If anyone says, "I love God," yet hates
his brother, he is a liar. For anyone who
does not love his brother whom he has seen,
cannot love God, whom he has not seen.*
1 John 4:20

Complete reconciliation to God is not possible without a willingness to be reconciled to others as well. Why? Because one of the clear commands in the Bible is that we be reconciled to others. And as long as we are not obeying God's scriptural commands, we are sinning—and thus not reconciled to Him. "If anyone says, 'I love God,' yet hates his brother, he is a liar. For anyone who does not love his brother whom he has seen, cannot love God, whom he has not seem" (1 John 4:20).

Frequently, I am asked, "Do you mean pray with *them?*" Aghast, they are wondering aloud how I could stoop to, and even defile myself by, praying together with Christians of different denominations or forms of worship.

At the International Prayer Assembly in Seoul, Korea in June 1984, I was asked to be on the committee writing the "International Call to Prayer" for the sponsoring Lausanne Committee on World

Evangelization. While discussing which Christians around the world we should call to prayer, the representative of a European country said, "If we include *them,* those praying in my country will throw this out."

Acting as secretary for this section, I became exasperated and inwardly horrified at such a discussion. Finally, facetiously yet firmly, I asked, "As I word this for the printer, should I include all those with whom we are going to spend eternity in heaven, or...." There was a long, shocked silence. Then all agreed with emphatic oneness that worldwide prayer is for all Christians. Blushing in shame, the European delegate apologized profusely. "I want the [people] to lift up holy hands in prayer, without anger or disputing" (1 Timothy 2:8).

> ➤ *Father, I'm sorry for living as if my broken relationships with people did not matter to You. Please forgive me. I promise to seek Christ and demonstrate the oneness He died to give us.*

When God Says No

*To God belong wisdom and power;
counsel and understanding are His.*
Job 12:13

I s it ever good when God says no? I had a meaningful no answer when we first moved to St. Paul. I was asked to be the vice-president of a large hospital auxiliary. I knew nothing about the two hospitals they served, but was assured it was a "You-won't-have-to-do-a-thing" job.

I immediately called back home to the prayer chains I had just left, asking them to pray for God's will. Soon the answer came from them and from others I had asked to pray; "God is saying no." And He was telling me no also.

When I told the committee what God had said, I almost felt the eyebrows being raised in surprise. I could not understand either why God would say no to such a great job when I was lonely with nothing to do in my new town.

A couple of weeks later, I found out why. The auxiliary president's husband was transferred out of state. Within two weeks, I would have been president of an organization that ran coffee shops and gift shops, and supervised volunteers and student candy stripers in two large hospitals. In addition, the whole work was needing to be reorganized—a process which was completed four years later. What a mess I would have made of that job!

"O dear God," I prayed, "Thank You for knowing the 'what ifs' and for keeping me from falling on my face."

> ➤ *Lord, Increase my faith in Your wisdom.*
> *Give me the ability to discern and the courage to*
> *accept Your "no" answers. I want to follow*
> *the path You have prepared for me.*

No Reconciliation to God
without It

Bear with each other and forgive whatever
grievances you may have against one another.
Forgive as the Lord forgave you.
Colossians 3:13

At the end of His earthly life, Jesus prayed to the Father in His High Priestly Prayer about the requirement that Christians be reconciled to one another. And as long as we are not reconciled to each other, we are sinning because we are disobeying this recorded desire of Jesus. And, of course, as long as there is sin in our lives, we are not reconciled to God. Jesus prayed:

I do not ask in behalf of these [whom the Father gave Him] alone, but for those also who believe in Me through their word; *that* they may all be one; even as Thou, Father art in Me, and I in Thee, *that* they also may be in Us; *that* the world may believe that Thou didst send Me. And the glory which Thou hast given me I have given to them; that they may be one, just as We are One; I in them, and Thou in Me, *that* they may be perfected in unity, *that* the world may know that

Thou didst send Me, and didst love them, even as Thou didst love Me (John 17:20-23, NASB, emphasis mine).

Contrary to popular thought, Jesus did not ask His children to be reconciled so that they *could become one,* but because they *were* one! So, whenever we pray asking God with which Christians we should pray, He answers, "But you are one!" "There is neither Jew nor Greek, slave nor free, male nor female, for you are all one in Christ Jesus" (Galatians 3:28).

But God's requirement for reconciliation is broader than just within the body of Christ. It includes *individual* reconciliation to mates, parents, in-laws, children, brothers, sisters, pastors, neighbors, employees, employers, competitors, and our enemies—all of whom may or may not be Christians. So, as long as we are not reconciled to even one of them, we are not obeying Jesus' plan for us. "Bear with each other and forgive whatever grievances you may have against one another. Forgive as the Lord forgave you" (Colossians 3:13).

> *Lord, Help me to make reconciliation as far as it is possible for me to do. I promise to pray for those who have despitefully used me. Thank You that Jesus insisted on the reconciliation of members of His body, not so that we could become one, but because we are one.*

Is Suffering Ever
God's Will?

*. . . if anyone suffers as a Christian, let him not
feel ashamed, but in that name let him glorify God.*
1 Peter 4:16, NASB

One year in our neighborhood Bible study we discovered a verse of Scripture which had a great impact on all of our lives. I knew the concept was scriptural, but I had never noticed it in God's Word before. "Therefore, let those also who suffer according to the will of God entrust their souls to a faithful Creator in doing what is right" (1 Peter 4:19, NASB).

Those who suffer according to God's will—is that in the Bible? Yes, it is. And almost everyone in our group that year was suffering. Of course, they weren't suffering because they were in the Bible study group (I hope). They were suffering in their bodies and in their spirits in various ways, but they began to see tremendous things take place. Whenever a problem arose, God would give us a specific answer immediately in His Word, and we would receive strength, grace, peace, maturity in Christ—whatever was needed.

Can suffering be God's will? Yes, we see it come

197

into focus in 1 Peter. If you're suffering read that epistle. It's tremendous. We, as Christians, aren't promised that we'll be free from suffering. Sometimes we suffer simply because we have frail, human bodies, but if we're committed to the God who doesn't ever make a mistake, we can have the assurance that He has permitted our suffering and *has a specific reason for it.*

➤ *Lord, Help me to understand that my suffering can be used as a tool to draw me closer to You.*

ALL THINGS FOR GOOD

*And we know that in all things God works
for the good of those who love Him, who have
been called according to His purpose.*
Romans 8:28

W ay back in our college days, I faced a crisis
when I lost my third pregnancy. I had already
had a miscarriage, then a full-term stillborn, and
now another miscarriage. "Lord, Lord, why all of
this?" my heart cried.

It was just after Word War II, and we had returned to college. In a burning bomber over Berlin,
Chris had promised God that he would become a
preacher after the war was over. Then God allowed
us to lose this third baby. Was He turning His back
and letting us suffer?

No, not at all. God gave me at that time Romans
8:28, "And we know that in all things God works
together for the good of those who love Him." I
loved God and Chris loved Him, and God had His
reasons for not allowing those three babies to live.

What all of God's reasons were I may never
know, short of eternity. But one thing God seemed
to tell me was, "Do you think that you and Chris
could have gone through seven more years of

schooling if you had had those three babies? Your dad had become an invalid and Chris' dad had died leaving two younger children. Could you have had the courage and the financial support to face seven more years of schooling with three babies to care for?"

Did God make a mistake? No. Not at all. Romans 8:28 has been our family's life verse ever since. We know that all things, absolutely everything, work together for our good. This was the omniscient God who never makes a mistake dealing in the lives of those who loved Him.

➤ *Dear Father, Give me the confidence to know that You are using all things in my life for my good.*

Make Restitution

The LORD said to Moses, ". . . When a man or woman wrongs another in any way and so is unfaithful to the LORD, that person is guilty and must confess the sin he has committed. He must make full restitution for his wrong. . . .

Numbers 5:6-7

Although God no longer hold us accountable to Himself for the sins He has forgiven, we still are responsible to the human beings we have hurt.

After praying, "God, I have sinned," and taking the steps of repenting and being reconciled to Him and others, are we absolved of all further responsibility and action? No. We still have a responsibility to the one against whom we have sinned.

This is the step of restitution. It is making amends, making good for a loss or damage. It is giving back to the rightful owner something that has been taken away. When we have sinned, it is our duty to make amends to the one victimized by our sinning.

While we must be reconciled to God when we sin, restitution is only made to the persons against whom we have sinned. There is no way we can repay God for violating His holiness. All we can do is repent because we have hurt Him so deeply and love Him so much that we will do everything in our power to restore our relationships with Him. Then we can serve Him with a new passion, making up for the lost days or opportunities. But our human relationships are different. Reconciliation to people against whom we have sinned or committed a crime usually includes making restitution of some kind.

➤ *O God, Forgive me for being insensitive to those I have hurt. Father, bring to my mind all those to whom I need to make restitution. God, I wait in silence for You to bring to mind the steps You want me to take.*

COMMITTED TO HIS WILL

"When he has brought out all his own,
he [the shepherd] goes on ahead of them,
and his sheep follow him because they know
his voice. . . . My sheep listen to My voice;
I know them, and they follow me."
John 10:4, 27

At our seminar session we invite participants at prayer time to commit their lives to God's perfect will. On a Wednesday morning, following such a session, one woman who attended committed her whole life, everything she held dear, to God's will. That very weekend her husband was killed in a motorboat accident! On the following Wednesday, one of the seminar members came with a message from this widow. "Please tell Evelyn that God prepared me for this experience when I committed my life to Him for His will last Wednesday."

Several months later at a prayer leaders' workshop, with tears in her eyes, she told us that she could really see God's will in this tragedy because one of her daughters who had turned away from Christ and left home had come back to Him, and was now taking her Daddy's place in leading the smaller children in Bible reading and prayer each day.

For you to do:

1. Think of the most important thing in the world to you. (It may be health, a loved one, a job, finances, schooling, etc.)

2. Now pray: Father, I want Your will in this thing that is most important in the world to me.

3. Now, in prayer, thank God for however He chooses to answer, knowing it is according to His perfect will.

4. Please don't pray the following prayer unless you really mean it:

> ➤ *Father, I want Your will in every area of my life including my job, my home, my health, my children, my loved ones, and my service for You. Amen.*

WHAT DO YOU EXPECT?

"Father, I have sinned against heaven and against you. I am no longer worthy to be called your son."
Luke 15:21

Prisoners often expect to be pardoned or paroled early after being sentenced regardless of the injury to their victims. But a pastor speaking at a recent National Religious Broadcasters convention made an important point when he said, "The criminal should stay in prison as long as the victim has to stay in the hospital."

A story I am told so frequently is that a husband leaves home, lives with another woman for a while, then comes back and acts as if nothing had happened. He feels as if he has a perfect right to expect all the comforts of home — just the way it was before. One woman told me that her husband comes and goes like this and becomes absolutely incensed if she so much as suggests that it may not be right and is hurting her.

Jesus told of a much more realistic expectation by the prodigal son who, after squandering his estate from his father in riotous living in a far country, came to his senses and went back home — expecting to be made just a hired hand. Even though his father embraced him and kissed him, the son cried, "Father, I have sinned against heaven and against you. I am no longer worthy to be called your son" (Luke 15:21).

We too should not expect to be welcomed back with open arms when we have caused grief and anxiety in someone. We should understand that the human response from our victim is more apt to be like that of the prodigal's elder brother who was angry and unwilling for a restored relationship. We should be extremely grateful when the victim is willing to forgive, accept us back, and restore our relationship.

> *Lord, There are many times when I need to be*
> *humbled. Give me a sensitive, loving heart*
> *toward those I have hurt, and help me not to*
> *take their forgiveness for granted.*

THANKS FOR...

Give thanks to the LORD, call on His name;
make known among the nations what He has done.
Psalm 105:1

The list of things for which I thank God in my prayers would fill many books, but here are just a few:

For redemption. Thanking God for transferring me out of the state of sin into which I was born into His glorious kingdom—forgiven and bound for eternity with my beloved Savior (Colossians 1:11-14).

For peace. Thanking God for the formula which has produced peace in my life. Here it is: "Be anxious for nothing, but in everything by prayer and supplication with thanksgiving let your requests be made known to God. And [then] the peace of God, which surpasses all comprehension shall guard your hearts and your minds in Christ Jesus" (Philippians 4:6, NASB).

For His omniscience. Although there are more than 5 billion people on Planet Earth, God the Father can give His undivided attention to each one of them all the time.

For Jesus' blood. Almost daily, I thank God that the blood of Jesus is the only positively irresistible force against evil (Revelation 12:10-11, NASB).

For setting me free. "If therefore the Son shall make you free, you shall be free indeed" (John 8:36, NASB).

For God using my body. For the progressively growing thankfulness of having given God my body in 1965, in that once-for-all action of Romans 12:1. I am thankful for the privilege of God using my still-living sacrifice in any way He chooses — to teach others the power of their prayers for me, that the words of God might be displayed in me (as in the man born blind whom Jesus healed), or to lead someone to Jesus in a redemptive way because of watching His power to transcend and use me through, and in spite of, physical weaknesses.

For you, dear prayer partners. I "do not cease giving thanks for you, while making mention of you in my prayers" (Ephesians 1:16, NASB).

> *I will praise You, O LORD, with all my heart;*
> *before the "gods" I will sing Your praise.*
> *I will bow down toward Your holy temple*
> *and will praise Your name*
> *for Your love and faithfulness,*
> *for You have exalted above all things*
> *Your name and Your word.*
> *When I called, You answered me;*
> *You made me bold and stouthearted.*
> *May all the kings of the earth praise*
> *You, O LORD,*
> *when they hear the words of Your mouth.*
> *(Psalm 138:1-4)*

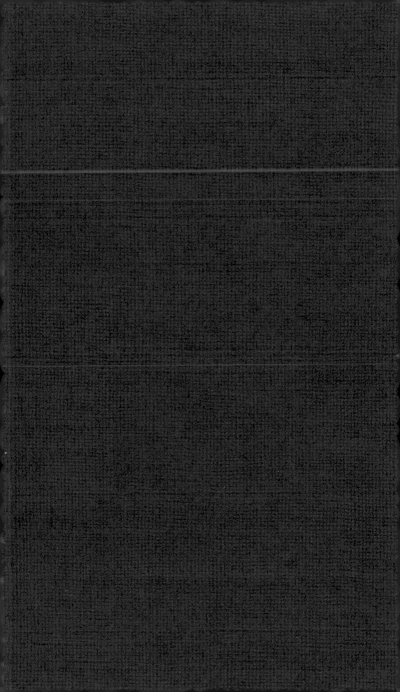